To Our Readers

Every day, there are times when you want to know more about something. It may be about how plants grow, or how electric motors work. You may want a certain fact about Abraham Lincoln, earth satellites, Bolivia, the invention of the piano, or what causes colds —to take just a few examples. Sometimes you need more information than a teacher, your parents, or a schoolbook can give. That's the time to turn to your GOLDEN BOOK ENCYCLOPEDIA.

This encyclopedia *is* for you. It has been made especially for readers who are starting to look up information on their own, and who want that information on their own bookshelf.

Into this encyclopedia have been put the most important facts of modern knowledge. The thousands of articles and color pictures, charts, diagrams, and maps make all this knowledge clear and exciting. Here is an endless parade of fascinating facts—facts you can depend upon for up-to-dateness and accuracy, because world-famous experts have checked them. Get into the habit of looking things up in your GOLDEN BOOK ENCYCLOPEDIA. Use it to discover more about interesting subjects mentioned in school. Let it be your partner in homework and school projects.

Watch newspapers and television for important news about science and government, foreign countries, famous people, sports, plants and animals, literature and art, weather and exploration. Look up these subjects in the index of your GOLDEN BOOK ENCYCLOPEDIA. Then read about them.

In the evening, or on a rainy day, pick up any volume of your GOLDEN BOOK ENCYCLOPEDIA. Open it anywhere and start reading. Notice how interesting just about any subject can be when it is clearly explained and well pictured. You will find yourself getting interested in more and more kinds of information.

THE GOLDEN BOOK ENCYCLOPEDIA is your guide to knowledge. The more you read it, the better you will like it.

THE EDITORS

THE GOLDEN BOOK ENCYCLOPEDIA

VOLUME II—ARTHUR TO BLOOD

In Sixteen Accurate, Fact-filled Volumes Dramatically Illustrated
with More Than 6,000 Color Pictures

THE ONLY ENCYCLOPEDIA FOR YOUNG GRADE-SCHOOL CHILDREN

ACCURATE AND AUTHORITATIVE

ENTERTAININGLY WRITTEN AND ILLUSTRATED TO
MAKE LEARNING AN ADVENTURE

by Bertha Morris Parker

*Formerly of the Laboratory Schools, University of Chicago
Research Associate, Chicago Natural History Museum*

GOLDEN PRESS · NEW YORK

CONTRIBUTORS AND CONSULTANTS

HALL BARTLETT, *Ed.D., Citizenship Education Project, Teachers College, Columbia University; Author*

WALT DISNEY, *Motion Picture and Television Producer*

EVELYN MILLIS DUVALL, *Ph.D., Author and Consultant on Family Life; Authority on Child Development*

EDNA E. EISEN, *Ph.D., Professor of Geography, Kent State University*

J. ALLEN HYNEK, *Ph.D., Associate Director, Smithsonian Astrophysical Observatory*

LELAND B. JACOBS, *Ph.D., Professor of Education, Teachers College, Columbia University*

ELEANOR M. JOHNSON, *M.A., Director of Elementary School Services, Graduate Division, Wesleyan University*

HERBERT A. LANDRY, *M.S., Ph.D., Director, Bureau of Educational Program Research and Statistics, New York City Public Schools*

MILTON LEVINE, *M.D., Associate Professor of Pediatrics, New York Hospital*

WILLY LEY, *Professor of Science, Fairleigh Dickinson University; Rocket Expert and Author*

NORMAN LLOYD, *M.A., Teacher of Literature and Materials of Music, Juilliard School of Music*

LENOX R. LOHR, *M.E., D.Eng., D.Sc., President, Museum of Science and Industry, Chicago*

WILL C. McKERN, *D.S., Former Director, Milwaukee Public Museum; Anthropologist*

RICHARD A. MARTIN, *B.S., Curator, N. W. Harris Public School Extension, Chicago Natural History Museum*

MAURICE PATE, *Executive Director, United Nations Children's Fund (UNICEF)*

NORMAN VINCENT PEALE, *D.D., LL.D., Litt.D., LH.D.; Minister, Marble Collegiate Church, New York; Author*

RUTHERFORD PLATT, *B.A., Member of Two North Pole Expeditions with Admiral MacMillan; Author of Nature Books*

ILLA PODENDORF, *M.S., Teacher of Science, University of Chicago Laboratory Schools; Author of Science Books*

MARY M. REED, *Ph.D., Supervisor of Little Golden Books; Formerly of Teachers College, Columbia University*

JOHN R. SAUNDERS, *M.A., Chairman, Department of Public Instruction, American Museum of Natural History*

GLENN T. SEABORG, *Ph.D., LL.D., D.Sc., Chancellor and Professor of Chemistry, University of California, Berkeley; Associate Director, University of California Radiation Laboratory; Co-winner of Nobel Prize for Chemistry, 1951*

LOUIS SHORES, *Ph.D., Dean of the Library School, Florida State University; Author and Authority on Reference Materials*

NILA BANTON SMITH, *Ph.B., Ph.D., Professor of Education and Director of The Reading Institute, New York University*

BRYAN SWAN, *M.S., Teacher of Physical Science, University of Chicago Laboratory Schools; Author*

SAMUEL TERRIEN, *S.T.M., Th.D., Auburn Professor of the Old Testament, Union Theological Seminary*

JESSIE TODD, *M.A., Formerly of the Art Department, University of Chicago; Art Lecturer; Contributor to Art Magazines*

LLOYD B. URDAL, *Ph.D., Assistant Professor, School of Education, State College of Washington*

JANE WERNER WATSON, *B.A., Editor and Author of More Than a Hundred Golden Books*

WILLIAM S. WEICHERT, *M.S., Supervisor of Science, Oakland (Calif.) Public Schools*

PAUL A. WITTY, *Ph.D., Professor of Education, Northwestern University; Specialist on Gifted Children*

STAFF

ROBERT D. BEZUCHA, *Project Director;* NORMAN F. GUESS, *Editorial Director;* R. JAMES ERTEL, *Managing Editor;* PAULINE NORTON, *Assistant Project Director;* ALICE F. MARTIN, *Associate Editor. Staff Editors:* GENEVIEVE CURLEY, JOAN FALK, HESTER GELB, RICHARD D. HARKINS.

© Copyright 1959 by Golden Press, Inc. Designed and produced by Artists and Writers Press, Inc. Printed in the U.S.A. by Western Printing and Lithographing Company. Published by Golden Press, Inc., Rockefeller Center, New York 20, N.Y.

Illustrations from GOLDEN BOOKS, published by Golden Press, Inc., New York, © 1946, 1949, 1951, 1952, 1953, 1954, 1955, 1956, 1957 by Golden Press, Inc.; from the Basic Science Education Series (Unitext), published by Row, Peterson and Company, Evanston, Illinois, © 1941, 1942, 1944, 1945, 1946, 1947, 1952, 1957, 1958, 1959, by Row, Peterson and Company; and from " '57 FORD CUSTOM AND CUSTOM 300," © 1956 Ford Motor Company, Dearborn, Michigan.

Arthur drew the sword from the anvil.

ARTHUR, KING The king of Britain was dead, and a new king was to be chosen. Merlin the Wise had driven a magic sword deep into an anvil of iron. The new king would be the one who could pull the sword from the anvil. A great tournament was to be held, and at the end of this tournament the drawing of the sword was to take place.

All the famous knights and nobles of Britain came to the tournament. One of the knights was Sir Kay. With him came his young foster brother Arthur.

During the tournament Sir Kay broke his sword. He sent young Arthur back to their pavilion to get another. But Arthur could not find one. Then he remembered seeing a sword in an anvil in front of the cathedral. He did not know that this sword was to decide the new king. He went to the anvil and drew out the sword easily. He took it to Sir Kay.

The new king promises to help his people.

Sir Kay saw at once what sword it was. He sent Arthur to their father, Sir Ector. Sir Ector knew then that Arthur would be the next king. But he went with the boy to put the sword back where he had found it. A few days later, after all the great knights and nobles had tried to draw the sword from the anvil without success, young Arthur was given a chance. He drew it out again, this time in front of them all.

This story of how Arthur became king of Britain is only one of many stories told about him. He was, all the stories tell, a wonderfully wise and good ruler. He brought together a band of brave knights who went about righting wrongs. In Arthur's castle they sat for meals at a big

Sir Gawain rode out for adventure.

round table, and so were called the Knights of the Round Table.

Lancelot was the bravest of all the Knights of the Round Table. Galahad was the most pure in heart. Other knights were Gawaine and Tristram, Pelleas and Percival, Gareth and Geraint. They all fought many battles for their king and had wonderful adventures.

Was there ever a King Arthur? No one knows for certain. Probably some of the tales are partly true. The first ones, it is thought, were told about a real king who ruled a part of Britain some 1,400 years ago. He was good, wise, and brave.

After the real king died, true stories were told about him. But many more were made up to show how great and good he was. In time no one knew which stories were true and which were not.

On the wall of a room in Winchester Castle in England there has hung for several hundred years the top of a great round table. It is 18 feet across. On its edge are the names of the Knights of the Round Table. But this table does not prove that the Knights of the Round Table were real people. Perhaps it was made by someone who liked the stories of King Arthur and wanted people to believe them. (See CASTLES; KNIGHTHOOD.)

ARTICLES OF CONFEDERATION

The 13 colonies that became the original United States of America fought through the Revolutionary War almost as 13 separate nations. They were only loosely joined by the Articles of Confederation, the first constitution of the United States.

The Articles of Confederation were drawn up in 1777, but they were not approved by all the colonies until 1781. Under the Articles, the country was ruled by a congress in which each state had one vote.

This congress had very little power. It could not collect taxes or make the states follow its orders. It could not enforce treaties with other nations. Any one colony—even the smallest—could block an action of the congress.

About all that the congress could do was to maintain an army and navy, manage the

The Constitutional Convention—1787

foreign affairs of the nation; set up post offices, and borrow money. The Articles of Confederation were designed to be a "league of friendship" among the states to help them fight their war for independence.

The Articles soon proved too weak for a big and growing country. Many people had little respect for the congress or its laws. There were many demands for a stronger central government.

In 1787 a Constitutional Convention met in Philadelphia with George Washington and Benjamin Franklin as two of its leaders. The Constitution they drew up went into effect in 1789 and ended the government under the Articles of Confederation. In spite of all their faults, the Articles were important to the colonies. They helped to bring them together, and showed that a union of states could work.

Washington and Franklin

ARTS The picture above shows three artists at work. One is painting a picture. He, of course, is a painter. The second is cutting a statue in stone. He is a sculptor. The third is carving a figure out of wood. He is a wood carver. Painting, sculpture, and wood carving are three of what we call the arts. Music, too, is one of the arts. So is acting. And there are many more.

There is no sharp line between the arts and some of the other things we do. Basketmaking, for instance, may be an art or it may not be. If a basketmaker is thinking only about making something that is big enough and strong enough to hold a bushel of potatoes, he is not an artist. But if he works a design into his basket or tries to give it a beautiful shape, he is an artist. In the same way, no one thinks he is an artist when he dances a square dance, but ballet dancing is an art. It is easy to see that printers, bookbinders, weavers, potters, and furniture makers may be artists or may not be.

No one knows which of the arts is oldest. We know that the cave men drew pictures on the walls of some of their caves. They carved the handles of some of their bone knives into the figures of animals. We know that the Egyptians and Babylonians planned and built beautiful buildings several thousand years ago. They decorated their pottery and wove beautiful cloth, too.

Music is also an ancient art. But how long ago people learned to make pleasant

Embroidery and needlepoint were arts practiced in colonial American homes.

sounds by beating on hollow logs and blowing through hollow reeds no one can tell. Dancing is an art that leaves no signs behind it. It may be the oldest art of all.

Among many early peoples art and religion were closely tied together. Some people believe that the pictures the cave men drew were prayers to their gods. Dancing is a part of the religion of many primitive peoples. Through the ages many of the most beautiful buildings have been temples or churches. Many of the most famous paintings and sculptures have been made for these temples and churches.

What people find around them in the places where they live has a great deal to do with how they try to bring beauty into

To be an artist a person must put into his work ideas of his own. He must not just copy the ideas of other people. It used to be that almost everyone who made something had a chance to be an artist. That time is gone. Now, in our age of machines, a workman usually has nothing to do with planning what he is making. He simply runs the machine which makes something someone else has planned.

In his work an artist often expresses some deep feeling. It may be joy or sorrow or fear. It may be a feeling of calm or excitement. It may be love of God or love of country or love of nature. The work of art should give the person who sees or hears it the same feeling. In this way the arts are

American Indians worshiped with music and dance.

The Egyptians used music in their worship.

their lives. The Eskimo carves beautiful figures out of the ivory from walrus tusks. But he does not plan big and beautiful buildings. With nothing but snow, driftwood, sod, and skins to use, he cannot build such buildings. In the same way, the Indians of the American Southwest make lovely silver jewelry set with turquoise. Silver and turquoise are available for these Indians to use.

All works of art are alike in one way. They all have some kind of design, or pattern. A ballet has a design just as truly as a picture has. A symphony is designed as carefully as a beautiful building.

In Colonial times some girls studied music.

SOUTHWEST SILVERSMITH

a kind of language—a language which is often easier for other peoples to understand than spoken words. (See ARCHITECTURE; BALLET; BASKETS; MUSIC; PAINTING AND PAINTERS; SCULPTURE; WOOD CARVING.)

ASBESTOS The name "asbestos" comes from a Greek word that means "will not burn." There is nothing surprising about a mineral that will not burn. Not many minerals will. But asbestos is different from most minerals in this way: it can be pulled apart into fine threads, or fibers. Sometimes it is called "mineral silk." Another name for it is "cotton stone."

Asbestos fibers can be twisted or woven or molded together. They can be made into rope or cloth or paper. They can be put into plaster or paint or cement.

Shingles on houses are often made of asbestos-cement. There is no danger that a roof covered with these shingles will catch on fire from a spark. Theaters have asbestos curtains. If a fire breaks out on stage, the curtain can be put down to keep the fire from spreading.

Neither heat nor electricity can travel easily through asbestos. Sheets of asbestos are wrapped around furnace pipes to keep the heat from escaping. Asbestos fibers may be put between walls to shut heat in. Asbestos may also be used around wires to keep electricity from going off the path it is supposed to follow.

Asbestos makes good automobile brake bands and clutch linings. These parts have to withstand great heat. Every year thousands of miles of asbestos bands are woven or molded for automobiles.

People have known about asbestos ever since the days of the ancient Greeks. In the Middle Ages the famous emperor Charlemagne had a tablecloth made of asbestos. To clean it he threw it into a fire. The fire burned off all the grease that had been spilled on it but did not damage the cloth itself. The Chinese were making cloth of asbestos in the days of Marco Polo. In those days people thought that salamanders could live in fire. Asbestos was sometimes called "salamander's wool."

Some asbestos is mined in the United States. But the United States uses a great deal more asbestos than it gets from its own mines. Canada is the largest producer. (See MARCO POLO.)

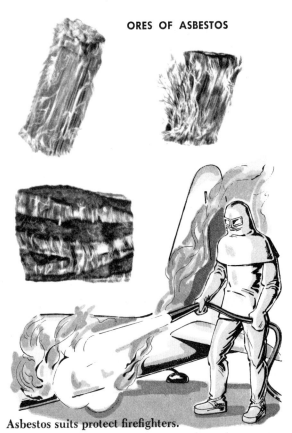

ORES OF ASBESTOS

Asbestos suits protect firefighters.

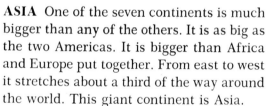

ASIA One of the seven continents is much bigger than any of the others. It is as big as the two Americas. It is bigger than Africa and Europe put together. From east to west it stretches about a third of the way around the world. This giant continent is Asia.

The eastern part of Asia is often spoken of as the Far East. Another name for it is the Orient. The part of Asia at the eastern end of the Mediterranean Sea is included in the region called the Near East. One part of the Near East is a peninsula sometimes called Asia Minor.

More than half of all the people in the world live in Asia. But its people are not scattered evenly over this big continent. Some parts of it are very crowded. There are many big cities. In wide stretches, however, there are almost no people at all. Finding out more about Asia will help to explain why this is so.

Asia stretches more than 5,000 miles from north to south. At its farthest north it reaches far beyond the Arctic Circle—up into the land of the midnight sun. Its southernmost tip almost touches the equator.

The "top" of Asia is so far north that it has very long, very cold winters. The people who live there have to endure temperatures of more than 50 degrees below zero. The

Asia is a continent of great contrasts. It has rich lands and poor lands; hot lands and cold lands. More than half the people of the world live in Asia.

The largest industrial region of China is in Manchuria.

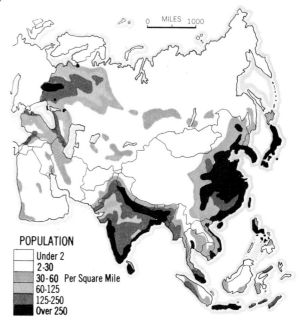

POPULATION

	Under 2
	2-30
	30-60 Per Square Mile
	60-125
	125-250
	Over 250

Hairy yaks are important beasts of burden in Tibet.

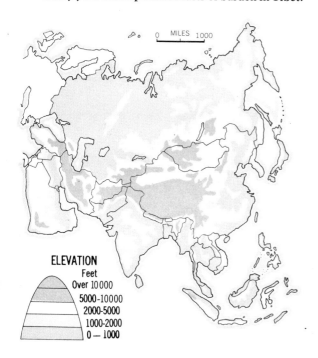

ELEVATION
Feet
Over 10 000
5000-10000
2000-5000
1000-2000
0 — 1000

story is very different for the parts of Asia that are near the equator. Here it is warm all the year round. At times it is almost unbearably hot. Temperatures of 125° F. have been recorded in southern India.

Some parts of Asia that are not far north are very, very cold in winter. They are cold because they are high above the sea. The Himalayas, the highest mountains in the world, are in Asia. More than 25 Asian peaks are higher than any peaks in the other six continents.

Asia also has land that is below the level of the sea. The lakes there are salty. The Dead Sea is one of them. Most of the land below sea level is desert.

There is other desert land, too. There are also great stretches of dry grassland. And some of the places where the weather is hot have so much rain that raising crops means fighting the jungle. In a single month 366 inches of rain once fell in a part of India.

As anyone would guess, the people in different parts of Asia live in homes that are very different. Some of them do not even have any real homes. They are nomads, or wanderers. They wander from place to place to find water and grass for their herds.

The hundreds of millions of people of Asia earn a living in many different ways. But most of them are either farmers or herders. Two of the greatest farming regions in the world are in Asia. One is in China. The other is in India. These regions are among the most crowded in the world.

In the big continent there are great stores of oil and other minerals. But many of the stores of minerals are still untouched.

Perhaps the first people lived in Asia. Many scientists think so. At least there were people in Asia a very long time ago. Three thousand years before Christ some of the people of Asia were highly civilized. These people lived in the Land between Two Rivers in western Asia. The rivers were the Tigris and the Euphrates. The Chinese were civilized long ago, too. So were the people of the Indus Valley in India.

The whole history of this great continent would take many books the size of this one. It would tell of conquering hordes and their leaders. It would tell about the rise and fall of great empires such as Babylonia and Persia. It would include the stories of the founders of great religions—Jesus, Mohammed, Confucius, and Buddha. It would tell of many inventions made in Asia and

People from many lands crowd the seacoast cities.

Modern farming methods are being used in parts of Asia.

People in the high Himalayas exchange goods by barter.

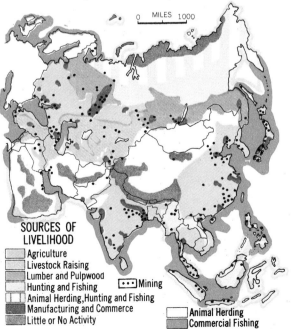

SOURCES OF
LIVELIHOOD

Agriculture
Livestock Raising
Lumber and Pulpwood
Hunting and Fishing
Animal Herding, Hunting and Fishing   Mining
Manufacturing and Commerce
Little or No Activity
Animal Herding
Commercial Fishing

The Chinese still keep many of their ancient customs.

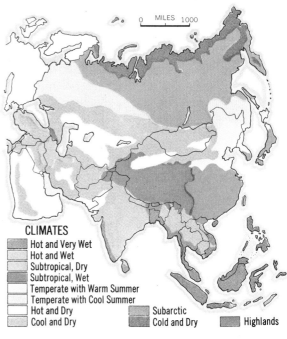

The temple of the Dawn is a famous temple in Thailand.

CLIMATES

Hot and Very Wet	
Hot and Wet	
Subtropical, Dry	
Subtropical, Wet	
Temperate with Warm Summer	
Temperate with Cool Summer	
Hot and Dry	Subarctic
Cool and Dry	Cold and Dry
	Highlands

The Great Wall of China was built about 2,000 years ago.

Temples nestle among great mountains in Tibet.

This great mosque is one of the sights of Turkestan.

carried from there to many other parts of the world.

Today Asia is divided into more than 30 countries. The people of these countries speak many different languages. They have different customs. They belong to several different races, too. The brown-skinned natives of India, the yellow-skinned Chinese, and the black-skinned pygmies of Malaya, for example, belong to quite different races.

Some of the countries of Asia are small. Lebanon, for instance, is only about half as big as New Jersey. About one and one-half million people live there. China, on the other hand, is a very big country. It has about 600 million people.

The great stretch of land across the north of Asia is often called Siberia. It is a part of the Soviet Union. The Asian part of the Soviet Union is larger than any other

Old style and modern dress are both seen in Asia.

country of Asia. It takes up more than a third of this biggest continent.

Asia is now in a period of unrest. Since World War II several countries have won their independence. Others have changed their form of government. More changes are sure to take place.

Seven hundred years ago Marco Polo traveled across Asia from the eastern end of the Mediterranean Sea to China. His trip was a wonderful adventure. It would still be a wonderful adventure today.

Suppose a traveler started at Jerusalem and traveled straight east to Shanghai. His trip would be 5,000 miles long. It would take him across eight countries. He would see some of the most barren land in the world and some of the most fertile. For a time he would be below the level of the sea. But he would also have to cross high Tibet. He would cross several great rivers. Parts of his journey would be dangerous. He might be attacked by bandits, for some of the regions he would cross are very wild. When he finally reached Shanghai he would be in the fourth-largest city of the whole world. (See ANGKOR; BABYLONIA; BRITISH EMPIRE; CHINA; FAR EAST; INDIA; JAPAN; NEAR EAST; PERSIA.)

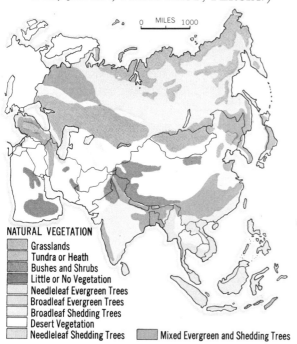

NATURAL VEGETATION
- Grasslands
- Tundra or Heath
- Bushes and Shrubs
- Little or No Vegetation
- Needleleaf Evergreen Trees
- Broadleaf Evergreen Trees
- Broadleaf Shedding Trees
- Desert Vegetation
- Needleleaf Shedding Trees
- Mixed Evergreen and Shedding Trees

India's gleaming Taj Mahal is world-famous.

The tiny kingdom of Nepal has many Hindu temples.

This is a temple to Buddha on the island of Ceylon.

Buildings of several religions are found in Israel.

ASPHALT In paving a street or building a road, men often use a black, tarlike material. The material is asphalt. Asphalt is also used in the making of roofing paper, shingles, tiles for flooring, and paints.

Asphalt is found in places where there is or used to be petroleum. It may flow slowly out of the ground and collect in pools. The asphalt that comes from the ground is called natural asphalt. Asphalt can also be made from petroleum.

When asphalt stands, it changes from a thick liquid to a soft solid. Chunks of asphalt are often found floating on the Dead Sea. In early times much asphalt was mined near this sea. Farther north, in Mesopotamia, the land between the Tigris and Euphrates rivers, there were many asphalt springs, too. The people in that region long ago cemented bricks together with asphalt to make pavements. They also sealed jars with asphalt.

There is a big asphalt lake on the island of Trinidad near the north coast of South America. This lake is about a mile across. In the center the asphalt is a liquid, but it is solid around the edges. Workers dig up the solid asphalt in chunks. Soon after a chunk of asphalt is taken out, the hole fills up again. There are smaller lakes like this in many places in the Americas.

The famous tar pits of California are pools of asphalt. In these pools scientists have found many wonderful fossils of mammoths, sabertooths, vultures, and other animals of the great Ice Age. So many fossils have been found in these pools that sometimes they are called "the deathtrap tar pools."

It is not hard to see how the deathtraps worked. After a rain, water covered the asphalt. Animals that waded out to get a drink became caught in the sticky substance and began to sink. Meat eaters—wolves and sabertooths—saw them and sprang on them. Then the meat eaters were caught, too.

ASTEROIDS The name "asteroid" means "starlike," but asteroids are actually little planets. They travel around the sun just as the big planets do. The paths of most of them are between the paths of Jupiter and Mars.

Giant animals were caught in the tar pits.

Ceres, the largest asteroid known, is 480 miles in diameter. Eros is 18 miles in diameter. Amor is only about a mile across. They are all too small to hold any air on them. They do not have enough gravity. There is so little gravity on Amor that, if a person could go there and could take a train with him, he could lift the train with one hand and swing it around his head.

About 1,500 asteroids have been discovered. New ones keep being found. Of course, these new ones are not really new. They have simply never been seen before. None of them can be seen without telescopes. Most of them have been discovered in pictures taken through telescopes.

The asteroid Hermes made a name for itself in 1937. It came very close to the earth on one of its trips around the sun. It was only 621,000 miles away!

No one knows surely how the asteroids were formed. One guess is that they came from a large planet which was once between Mars and Jupiter. Perhaps the large planet came too close to the giant Jupiter and was pulled to pieces.

Sometimes asteroids are called planetoids. Planetoids is really a better name, for these small bodies do not shine by their own light as stars do.

ASTROLOGY Another name for astrology is "stargazing." Long ago it was the custom in some countries to call in an astrologer when a baby was born. The astrologer "read the stars" and from them told the baby's fortune. He told whether the child would grow up to be brave or timid, strong or weak, rich or poor. "Reading the stars" meant chiefly seeing where the planets were among the stars. Astrologers predicted such things as wars and famines, too. For centuries there was an astrologer in the court of almost every king.

Astrology is not a science. The stars, scientists agree, have nothing to do with the fortunes of people or nations. The astrologers of old predicted many things that never came true. But even now many people believe in astrology.

Astronomy *is* a science. It is the true study of the stars. It is an old science. But many of the early astronomers had to make their living by practicing astrology.

An Astrologer
"Reading the Stars"

ASTRONOMY Astronomy is the study of the sun, the moon, the stars, the planets, and all the other heavenly bodies. It is a very old science.

No one person found out all that we know now about the sky. Down through the centuries thousands of people have made discoveries. Some of these discoveries are so important that the people who made them are famous. These are a few of the most famous astronomers:

Hipparchus (190-120 B.C.) was a Greek. He made the first star catalogue. A star catalogue is a list of stars which tells where each one is in the sky.

Ptolemy (A.D. 100-170) was also a Greek. He made a list of constellations, or groups of stars. The 48 constellations he named did not cover the whole sky, but no one dared add to the list for more than a thousand years. Ptolemy thought that the earth stood still and that all the heavenly bodies traveled around it. Of course, this idea was wrong, but many of his ideas were right. An astronomy book he wrote was used for centuries.

Copernicus (ko PER ne kus) (1473-1543) was a Polish astronomer. He wrote a book that completely changed the study of astronomy. In it he explained that the earth is not the center of the universe. He said that the earth is one of the sun's family of planets and that it spins on its axis as it travels around the sun. All the astronomers of today agree with those ideas.

Tycho Brahe (BRAH e) (1546-1601), a Dane, was the first astronomer to study the stars called "novae." Novae are stars that suddenly become very much brighter and then fade. Brahe also watched the planets and kept a careful record of where they were in the sky.

Johannes Kepler (1571-1630) was a German. He set for himself the task of finding out whether the paths of the planets were perfect circles. With the help of Tycho Brahe's careful records, he discovered that they were not. Instead, they are flattened circles, or ellipses (e LIP sez).

Galileo (1564-1642), the famous Italian scientist, was the first to study the sky with a telescope. He discovered that there are mountains on the moon and sunspots on the sun. He saw four of the moons of Jupiter.

Christian Huyghens (HOY kens) (1629-1695) was a Dutch astronomer. He discovered the rings of Saturn and found out a great deal about Mars.

Sir Isaac Newton (1642-1727), the most famous English scientist of all time, wondered what keeps the moons and planets in their paths. In trying to find out, he discovered the laws of gravity and motion.

Edmund Halley (1656-1742) lived in England in Newton's time. He became famous for his study of comets. Halley's comet is named for him.

Among the great names in astronomy since Halley's time are Herschel, Laplace, and Lowell. Today's many astronomers, helped by wonderful new instruments, are steadily adding to our knowledge of the universe. (See MOON; PLANETS; SOLAR SYSTEM; STARS.)

ATHLETICS Many boys and girls look forward to being good athletes. Almost every high school and college in the United States has its baseball and basketball teams. Many have football and tennis teams. All over the United States there are track and field meets every year. These meets are contests in running, jumping, pole vaulting, and throwing. There are swimming meets, too. Athletics are very much a part of our schools today. Many a boy or girl is just as proud of being a good athlete as of being a good student.

It was not at all the same a hundred years ago. Then most people would have called athletics in school a waste of time. They did not think that boys and girls should take the time away from their studies for running and jumping and playing games.

But the idea of athletics is not new. More than 2,000 years ago the Greeks said that it was just as wise to train the body as to train the mind. They urged people to develop a sound mind and a healthy body. They started the famous Olympic games. But for many centuries the Greek idea was forgotten.

There is more to athletics than just building a strong body. Such activities help people learn to be good winners and good losers. They help them learn how to get along well with others. And, of course, they are fun.

Nowadays many people enjoy athletics so much that they do not give them up when they leave school. In cities there are many gymnasiums that are open to the public and many athletic clubs.

In athletic meets careful records are kept. Every once in a while a newspaper headline tells that some record has been broken. The chart below gives a few of to-day's records. (See GAMES AND SPORTS.)

OFFICIAL ATHLETIC RECORDS					
Event	Record	Date	Event	Record	Date
100 yard dash	9.3 sec.	1948	High jump	7 ft. 1⅛ in.	1957
220 yard dash	20.0 sec.	1956	Pole vault	15 ft. 8¼ in.	1957
440 yard dash	45.7 sec.	1958	Running broad jump	26 ft. 8¼ in.	1935
1 mile run	3 min. 57.2 sec.	1957	Hop, step and jump	54 ft. 3¾ in.	1955
1 mile relay race	3 min. 7.3 sec.	1956	16 lb. shot-put	63 ft. 1¾ in.	1956
120 yard hurdles	13.4 sec.	1956	16 lb. hammer throw	225 ft. 4 in.	1958
220 yard hurdles	22.1 sec.	1958	Discus throw	194 ft. 6 in.	1953
440 yard hurdles	49.7 sec.	1958	Javelin throw	281 ft. 2¼ in.	1956

Golf — Swimming (diving) — Basketball — Football — Bowling — Ice Skating — Skiing — Archery — Tennis — Boxing — Wrestling — Baseball — Track — Javelin throw — Hockey — ATHLETICS

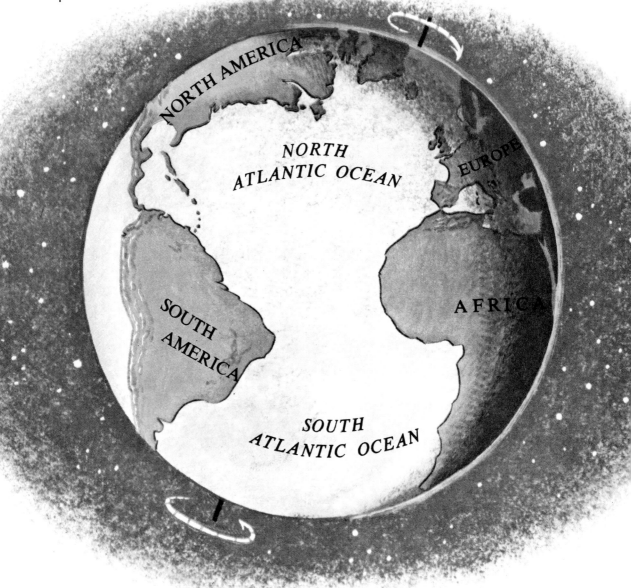

ATLANTIC OCEAN The Atlantic Ocean is one of the oceans that separate the Old World from the New. For centuries it kept the Americas from being discovered by the people of Europe.

Many wrong ideas about the Atlantic made early sailors unwilling to sail far out into it. One idea was that it reached out to "the edge of the world." Sailors were afraid that they might sail right off the earth. Another idea was that at the equator the ocean would be boiling hot.

The Atlantic Ocean is only half as big as the Pacific, but it is still very large. It is more than 4,000 miles wide where Colum-bus crossed it. Even at its narrowest it is about 2,000 miles wide. This narrowest place is between the bulge of South America and the bulge of Africa.

Two things make the Atlantic Ocean rather unusual. For so large an ocean it has very few islands. It is, moreover, the world's saltiest ocean.

There is so much water in the Atlantic that it is hard to imagine how much there is. But suppose no more rain fell into it and no more water was brought to it by rivers. It would take the ocean about 4,000 years to dry up. On the average the water is a little more than two miles deep, but in

NORTH AMERICA   AZORES   GIBRALTAR
                                                                SÃO MIGUEL

PROFILE OF THE ATLANTIC OCEAN FLOOR

places it is much deeper. The deepest spot is near Puerto Rico. This "deep" measures 30,246 feet—almost six miles.

One of the longest mountain ranges of the world rises from the floor of the Atlantic. This mountain range runs north and south down the middle of the ocean. The tops of a few of the mountains reach up above the sea and make islands. The Azores are the tops of peaks in this mid-Atlantic mountain range.

Several hundred miles eastward from Florida there is a part of the ocean called the Sargasso Sea. Here the water is quiet, for there is little wind. In the days of sailing vessels crews were afraid they would be becalmed here. Sometimes they were. The sea gets its name from sargassum, a kind of seaweed that is brought in from far and wide by ocean currents.

Ocean currents are sometimes called "rivers in the sea." One of these "rivers" in the Atlantic is called the Gulf Stream. It is a current of warm water. Another is the Labrador current — cold water coming down from the Arctic. Ocean currents affect the climates of the lands near which they flow.

The Atlantic furnishes much food for the people on its shores. One of its most famous fishing regions, the Grand Bank, is near Newfoundland.

Today the Atlantic is a great highway. It is not, however, always a smooth and safe one. Storms sweep across it and pile up great waves. Icebergs float down from the Far North across the paths of ships.

We now have such fast ways of traveling that this big ocean seems to have grown smaller. Columbus sailed for more than two months to cross it. A fast modern steamship can make the trip in less than four days. Airplanes fly from New York to London in only ten hours and from South America to Africa in four! (See CONTINENT, LOST; GULF STREAM; OCEANS.)

Fishing boats of many kinds go out on the waters of the Atlantic every day.

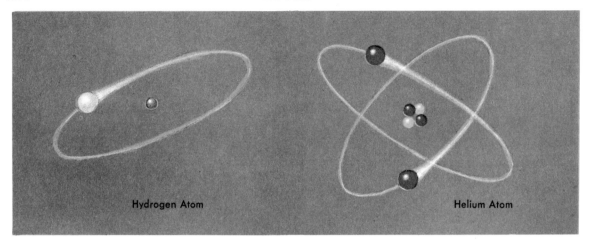

Hydrogen Atom   Helium Atom

ATOMS All the millions of substances in the world are built out of only about a hundred simple substances. We call these simple substances elements. The very smallest bit of an element is an atom. Iron, for instance, is one of the elements. The very smallest bit of iron is an atom of iron.

Atoms are so tiny that it is hard to imagine how tiny they are. The ink in the period at the end of this sentence has more atoms in it than there are people in the whole world. In a thimbleful of air there are more atoms than you could count if you lived to be a million years old. Of course, atoms are too small to be seen even with powerful microscopes. We know about them only from the way they act.

There can be millions of different substances because atoms of different kinds can join together in different ways. Atoms of oxygen and atoms of hydrogen, for instance, can join to form water. They can join in different proportions to form hydrogen peroxide.

Scientists have a way of writing the names of substances so that it is easy to tell what kinds of atoms the substances have in them and how the numbers of the different kinds of atoms compare. The scientists' way of writing water is H_2O. H stands for hydrogen, O for oxygen. The 2 shows that there are two atoms of hydrogen for every atom of oxygen. Hydrogen peroxide is written H_2O_2.

Atoms are so small that it is almost unbelievable that anything could be smaller. But atoms are made up of even smaller particles. Every atom has a center, or nucleus. The nucleus of an atom always has in it one or more particles called protons. In the case of every element except hydrogen it has particles called neutrons in it, too. Traveling around the nucleus there are one or more tiny particles called electrons.

The World's First Atomic Submarine, the U.S.S. Nautilus

The atoms of a few rare elements gradually break down by themselves. They shoot out some of the particles they are made of. As they do, they give off energy, mostly in the form of heat and light. These elements, we say, are radioactive. Radium is one of them. Uranium is another.

Not many years ago scientists found a way of splitting atoms artificially and making them give off energy. They used machines called "atom smashers" to hurl parts of atoms against the nucleus of an atom with so much force that it would split the nucleus. The splitting of atoms is called atomic fission.

After they found out how an atom can be split, scientists found out how to use the splitting of one atom to set off the splitting of other atoms. They discovered, in other words, how to bring about a chain reaction. Soon afterward the first atom bomb was made. When an atom bomb explodes, many of the atoms in it are split. The energy they give off does a terrible amount of damage.

In atomic fission it is the nucleus that is split. For this reason, atomic energy is often called nuclear energy.

Now scientists have found how to control the splitting of atoms. They have worked out ways of making atomic fission supply a steady amount of energy and serve mankind. So far scientists have done most of their experimenting with uranium. Some power stations are already using atomic energy to generate electricity for homes

and factories. And there are now submarines which operate on atomic energy.

Scientists have also found out how to produce atomic energy by making atoms of hydrogen fuse together. Atomic fusion is going on constantly in the sun. It gives us the light and heat that make life on earth possible. Atomic fusion gives hydrogen bombs their terrible destructive power. Perhaps in time scientists will be able to tame the energy from fusion for peacetime uses. (See ELEMENTS; MOLECULES; RADIUM; URANIUM.)

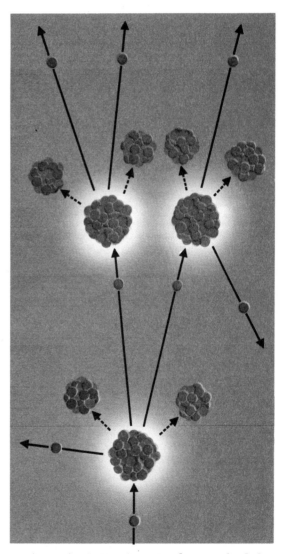

A uranium atom is as touchy as a loaded mousetrap. Particles from a splitting uranium atom strike other atoms and cause them to split. Particles from those atoms hit other atoms. The chain reaction spreads rapidly.

Imagine a room full of mousetraps loaded with ping-pong balls. If one of the traps is set off, balls will fly through the air and set off other traps. Now more balls fly out and set off more traps.

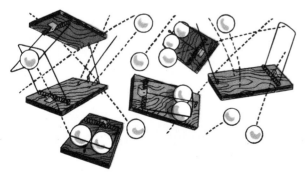

Attila's horde overran Europe.

ATTILA (AT i la) (406-453) In 433 Attila and his brother Bleda became joint rulers of the Huns, wild tribes living in southeastern Europe. Eleven years later Attila had Bleda killed. Then he set out on a march of conquest. After conquering lands to the east and south, he started westward. Attila was so cruel a warrior that he was known as the "scourge of God."

At first his army swept everything before it. But Flavius Aetius (AY tee us), a great Roman general, joined forces with Theodoric, the king of the Visigoths, and met Attila and his army at Châlons (shuh LAWN). The fighting was so fierce that legends say the dead warriors continued the battle in the sky. About 250 thousand men were killed. In the end Attila was defeated.

In 453 Attila was preparing to march on Italy. But suddenly, just before his troops were ready to set out, he died.

The body of Attila was put in a coffin of gold. The gold coffin was put in a coffin of silver. The silver coffin was put in a coffin of iron. Men were sent to bury Attila. When they came back they were killed. No one must ever know Attila's burial place!

AUDUBON, JOHN JAMES (1785-1851) Audubon's name is one of the great names in the story of American art. He is world famous for his lifelike paintings of American birds.

There is a great deal of mystery about Audubon's early life. No one is sure where he was born. No one is sure, either, who his parents were. Audubon called himself by different names at different times and thus added to the mystery.

The part of Audubon's story we know surely about begins in France in 1794. In that year he was adopted by a French naval captain named Audubon. Captain Audubon and his wife were very kind to the boy. They sent him to school, hoping that he would be a soldier or an engineer. But he was more interested in wandering in the woods and drawing pictures of the animals he saw. When he was 18 he came to the United States.

Young Audubon was charming and soon had many friends in America. He tried one way after another of making a living. He taught French and dancing, kept a store, ran a mill, and painted portraits. But his real interest was in painting the birds and other animals he saw.

We owe his beautiful pictures partly to Lucy Bakewell, the girl he married. For she worked as a governess to give him a chance to paint. The hundreds of pictures he painted are now very valuable. The Audubon Society, made up of people much interested in birds, was named in his honor.

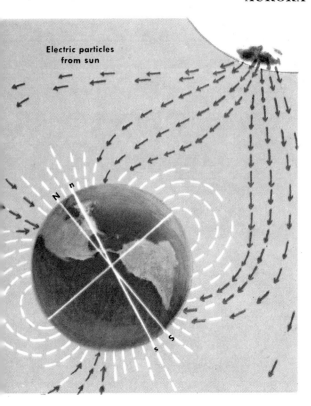

Electric particles from sun

AURORA BOREALIS (bo ree AY lis)
The sky in the picture at the right is lighted
up by the beautiful northern lights. Another name for them is aurora borealis.

For a long time the northern lights were
a great puzzle. The people of olden times
made up many stories to explain them. One
of these was that the light came from a
battle the gods were fighting. In more recent times people have thought the aurora
was sunlight reflected from the snow and
ice in the Far North.

The right explanation, scientists tell us,
is this: On the sun there are often great
storms. We call them sunspots. From these
sunspots, streams of tiny electric particles
are shot out. When these particles reach
the upper air, they cause the aurora. The
different colors come from the effect of the
electric particles on the different gases in
the air. The colors are produced very much
as colors are produced in neon signs.

The northern lights are at their best in
the Far North. But they have been seen
from all over the United States and Europe.

A good time to look for them is on a night
when radio programs are not coming in
well. For the particles that cause the northern lights also interfere with radio.

In the Far South there are lights like the
northern lights. They are called the aurora
australis. (See SUNSPOTS.)

Electric particles stream out from sunspots
on the sun toward the north and south poles
of the earth.

When these electric particles strike the
earth's atmosphere, they cause it to glow in
fingers of light in both the North and South
Polar regions.

AUSTRALIA Only one country in the world fills a whole continent. That country is Australia. The continent it fills is Australia, too. Australia, then, is both a country and a continent.

Australia is the only continent except Antarctica that is all south of the equator. Its name means "southland." Since it is south of the equator, its seasons are just the opposite of ours. It has summer while we have winter, and the other way around.

Sometimes Australia is called the "Island Continent." There is a good reason why. It *is* an island. It is 2,000 miles from the mainland of Asia and almost halfway around the world from Europe. More than 6,000 miles of ocean separate it from the Americas.

Two hundred years ago there were no white people in Australia. A hundred years earlier Dutch sailors had stopped at several places on the northern and western coasts. They had brought back word that the land was "of very little use." It is no wonder that they had that idea. The northern shores of Australia are near enough to the equator to be very hot. They get a great deal of rain. The hot, wet climate is one that white people cannot stand well. Much of the western coast is dry and barren. There is a great desert in Australia, and it comes down to the sea on the western coast.

William Dampier was the first Englishman to reach Australia. But Captain James Cook's explorations of the southeast coast in 1770 were more important. There he found a pleasant climate. He found beautiful forests, too. On the shores of one bay he saw so many kinds of strange plants that he named it Botany Bay. When he took back word of this pleasant new land, Britain claimed it. Not long afterward people from Britain began to settle there. They settled not far from where the city of Sydney now stands.

The settlers soon discovered that many of the animals as well as the plants of Australia were unlike those found anywhere else. Among the animals were kangaroos and wombats and koalas. They carry their babies in pouches. There were emus, kookaburras, black swans, and other odd birds, too.

The early settlers on the east coast were shut in between mountain and sea. For years they could not make their way across the mountains. When they did, they found great stretches of grassland.

Some of the early settlers had been sheepmen in Britain. They saw that the grasslands would be a wonderful place for raising sheep. They knew that wool stands shipping well. They knew, too, that it is worth enough to pay for shipping it long distances. Many started sheep ranches. Before long Australia became the greatest wool-producing country in the world.

In some cases cattle were raised on the grasslands instead of sheep. But beef and butter are not so easy to ship as wool.

About a hundred years ago gold was discovered in southeastern Australia. There was a great gold rush. Thousands of people went to the new land to find their fortunes.

Australian natives have no villages and wear no clothes. They live by hunting—and they are very good at it. For weapons, they use long spears and boomerangs. Most of them do not like civilization, but some now work on cattle ranches.

Gold was discovered in Australia at about the same time as the great gold rush in California. Gold mining is now an important industry in Australia. It has been estimated that the country's total gold production is about $5,600,000,000.

There are thousands of beef and dairy cattle in Australia. Much more beef, butter, and cheese are produced than the people of the country need. What is left over is shipped to other nations. Most of the excess goes to Great Britain.

Koala

Dingo

Black Swan

Wombat

Duckbill

Australia has strange animals found nowhere else in the world. The dingo is a wild dog that preys on sheep. Hunters get paid for killing dingos. Koala bears are friendly little animals. They spend their lives in trees and eat only eucalyptus leaves. The duckbill, or platypus, is a real freak. It has a bill like a duck even though it is a mammal. It lays eggs. The wombat is a burrowing animal with thick, coarse fur. The only swans found in Australia are black. All black swans came originally from Australia.

Australia's greatest industry is sheep raising. There are 126,000,000 sheep there, more than 13 times the number of people in the country. Australia produces about one-third of all the world's wool.

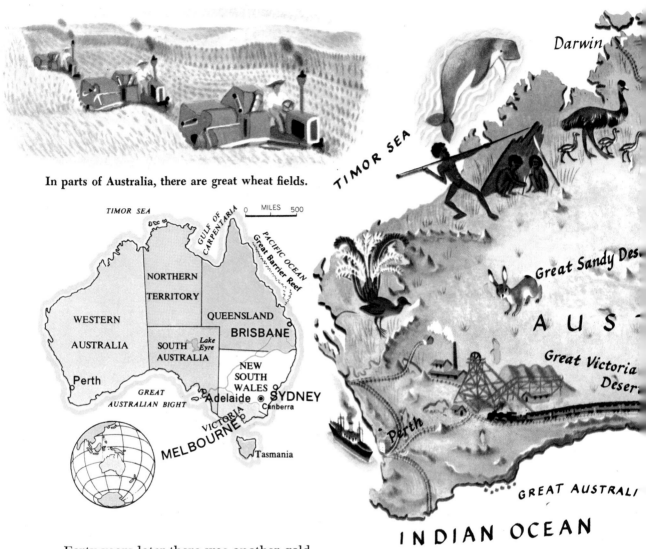

In parts of Australia, there are great wheat fields.

Forty years later there was another gold rush. This time gold was discovered in the west. The first miners there had a hard time. Water was very scarce. There were no railroads to bring in supplies and carry the gold away. There were not even any good roads. But a railroad was built. The west was joined with the east. Soon afterward—on Jan. 1, 1901—all the separate parts of Australia united into one country.

Many of the people who came to Australia to find gold stayed on to do other kinds of work. They found that Australia has other riches. It has coal and copper and lead and zinc. The forests have much good timber. Along the seashores pearl shell and tortoise shell can be gathered. Some of the land proved to be good for wheat. Other land proved to be good for sugar cane or for fruit orchards.

Of course, people were needed to buy and sell what was raised. Others were needed to manufacture such things as butter, cheese, flour, steel, farm machinery, mining tools, shoes, and clothing. Cities grew.

Even today the big country is far from crowded. It is about the size of the United States, but it has less than three times as many people in it as there are in Chicago. More than half of all the people of the country live in its cities. Sydney and Melbourne are the two largest.

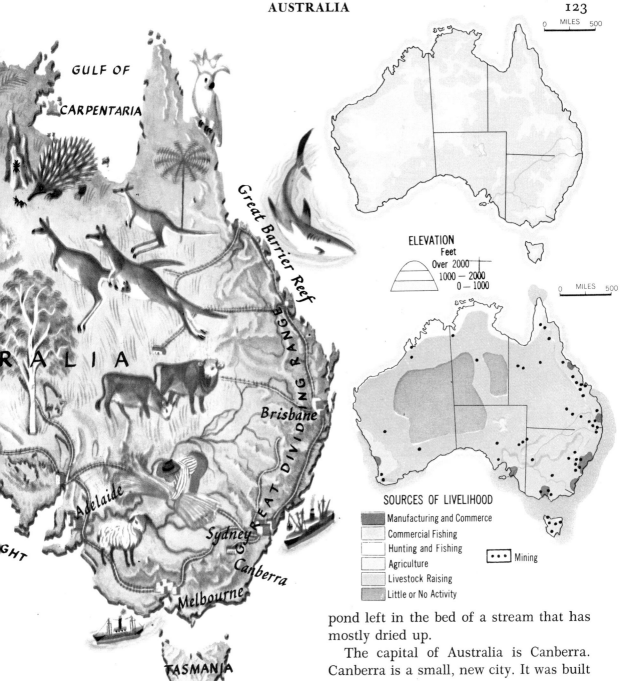

0 MILES 500

ELEVATION
Feet
Over 2000
1000 — 2000
0 — 1000

0 MILES 500

SOURCES OF LIVELIHOOD

Manufacturing and Commerce
Commercial Fishing
Hunting and Fishing
Agriculture
Livestock Raising
Little or No Activity

Mining

Australia is still closely tied to its mother country. It is a free country, but it belongs to the British Commonwealth of Nations.

The people of Australia speak English. But some of their words are not found in the English of either America or Britain. "Burster" and "billabong," for instance, are two words that Australians use. A burster is a sudden strong wind. A billabong is a pond left in the bed of a stream that has mostly dried up.

The capital of Australia is Canberra. Canberra is a small, new city. It was built just to be the capital of the country. When the government of Australia decided to build a new city for a capital, a contest was held for a plan for the city. An American won the contest.

Airplanes have now cut down the travel time from Australia. Refrigerator boats make it easy in these days to ship meat, butter, and even fruit to faraway markets. But Australia's great distance from other lands is still a handicap. (See SYDNEY.)

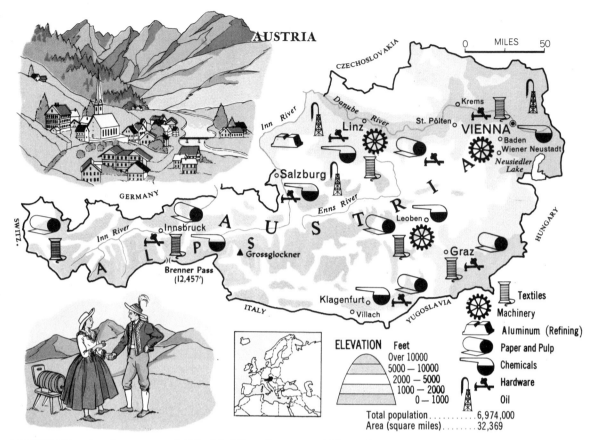

AUSTRIA

Total population...........6,974,000
Area (square miles)........32,369

ELEVATION Feet
Over 10000
5000 — 10000
2000 — 5000
1000 — 2000
0 — 1000

Textiles
Machinery
Aluminum (Refining)
Paper and Pulp
Chemicals
Hardware
Oil

AUSTRIA At the start of World War I Austria was a part of Austria-Hungary, a big and powerful country. More than 50 million people lived there. It contained all the land that is now in the two countries of Austria and Hungary. It contained, too, a great deal of land that is now divided among other countries. Austria-Hungary was rich because of its farms and factories and minerals. Many trade routes passed through it. The Danube made a great river highway across it. There were land routes across it, too. Its capital, Vienna, was one of the world's great cities. It was a center of trade and a center of culture, too.

At the end of World War I, Austria was separated from Hungary. Part of Czechoslovakia was carved out of its land. So was a part of Yugoslavia. Austria lost land to Italy and Poland, too. It lost its best farmland, most of its minerals, and most of its factories. It became a small, weak country.

Today Austria is about the size of the state of Maine. Most of it is mountainous. Like its neighbor Switzerland, it is an inland country. It does not touch the sea.

Although Austria is only as large as Maine, it has as many people as the states of Maine, New Hampshire, Vermont, and Massachusetts combined. It is not easy for so many people to make a living in so small a country.

About a fourth of all the people in Austria live in Vienna. Vienna is no longer the great center of trade it once was, but many of its people still earn their living by buying and selling. It has factories, too, where such things as paper, cloth, and tools are made. Many Austrians outside the city are farmers. Some of their farms are on steep mountain slopes. Much of the mountain land is covered with forests. These forests also give work to many. The forests yield lumber, wood pulp, turpentine and resin.

Austria's mountains make a wonderful vacation spot. The beautiful scenery is much like the scenery of Switzerland. Every year thousands of tourists go to Austria. The tourist trade is Austria's third-largest industry. It is helping to make Austria a prosperous country. (See DANUBE; HUNGARY; VIENNA.)

Cugnot
1769

Benz's Gasoline-powered Automobile

AUTOMOBILES As recently as 50 years ago all the members of a family would run to the window to watch an automobile pass. They watched the "horseless carriage" to see if it could climb the next hill. They wondered what would happen to the passengers in a rain storm. People joked about the early cars, but almost everybody wanted to own one.

The automobiles of 50 years ago did not look much like the cars of today. They looked more like the horse-drawn buggies and carriages people were used to riding in. Some of the early cars even had sockets for buggy whips.

The idea of using an engine of some kind to turn the wheels of a carriage is really quite old. The first automobile accident happened in 1769, nearly 200 years ago. A steam carriage built by the Frenchman Nicolas Cugnot (Kune YO) overturned on a curve. It was traveling less than three miles an hour!

In 1831 steam carriages carrying 18 passengers were making regular trips between cities in England. They averaged about five miles an hour. But toll road keepers began raising their rates on steam carriages. People sometimes threw stones at the carriages. The government also began passing laws against them. One of these laws, called the Red Flag law, said that a man

had to walk in front of any steam carriage and carry a red flag during the day or a red lantern at night. All these factors kept the steam carriages from becoming very popular in England.

In Germany, a few years later, men developed new ideas about engines. Nikolaus Otto made an engine in 1876 that worked very much like a modern gasoline engine. In 1885 Gottlieb Daimler successfully mounted a small model of this engine on a bicycle. This engine burned kerosene. In that same year another German, Karl Benz, built a three-wheel car that was driven by a gasoline engine. The modern car grew out of many of these older ideas.

The first gasoline car in the United States was built in 1892 by Charles and Franklin Duryea of Springfield, Mass. It was a buggy with a two-cylinder engine fastened to the back axle. The Duryeas were not satisfied with this car, however, and the next year they made a better one. Very soon afterward Elwood Haynes, R. E. Olds, Henry Ford, and others had built cars.

In the early days of automobiles, car builders tried mostly to build a car that would work. By 1912, builders could make cars that would run fairly well. They now began to look for different ways to improve their cars.

The job of making cars better has been going on for many years. Many changes have been made over the years. Most of the old ideas are still being used, however, in a changed form.

Duryea
1893

Mercedes-Benz
1958

Several thousand parts have to work together to keep a modern automobile running properly. The picture at the bottom of the page shows some of these parts.

A fuel pump brings gasoline from the gas tank and pumps it into the carburetor. The carburetor is a mixer that mixes air and gasoline together into a fine mist. The air comes into the carburetor through a filter, which strains out dust and dirt. About 2,000 gallons of air are mixed with each gallon of gasoline.

The air and gasoline mist is sent to the cylinders of the engine. These cylinders are like big tubes closed off at the top. The air-gasoline mist gets into the cylinder through a valve, which works like a one-way trap-door at the top of the cylinder.

In the lower part of each cylinder is a plunger, called a piston, which moves up and down. The piston moves up and compresses the air-gas mixture. At just the right moment, a hot, electric spark jumps across the prongs of the spark plug near the top of the cylinder. This spark makes the air-gas mixture explode. The explosion forces the piston down very hard. The bottom of the piston of each cylinder is connected to a shaft called a "crankshaft." When the cylinder pistons are forced down, one after the other, they make the crank-

shaft go around. The turning of this shaft is what makes the wheels go around.

The turning force created by the explosions in the engine is sent to the wheels through the transmission. There are several gears in the transmission. "Low gear," which is the most powerful gear, is used for the difficult job of getting the car started. "Second gear" is used for picking up more speed, and "high gear" is used for regular driving.

In many cars, the driver shifts from one gear to another by moving a lever near the steering wheel. In other cars, the work of shifting from one gear to another is done automatically.

A long shaft carries the turning motion from the transmission back to another set of gears called the "differential." A separate shaft goes from the differential to each of the two rear wheels. The differential makes it possible for one of the rear wheels to go faster than the other one when the car is going around a corner.

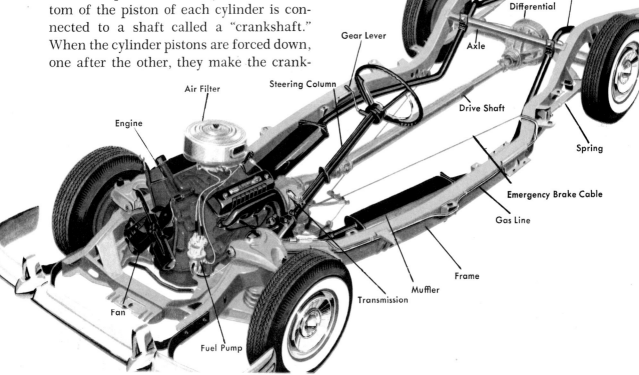

In most cars, only the rear wheels are made to turn by the engine. The front wheels, connected to the steering wheel, are used to guide the car.

The explosions that take place in the engine create a great deal of heat. This heat would ruin the engine if something weren't done about it. Water is pumped around the engine to keep it cool. The water is then sent to the radiator, which is mounted in front of the engine. The big fan at the front of the engine sucks air past the radiator to cool the water.

While the engine is running, oil is also being constantly pumped through it. The oil goes to the moving parts to keep them from wearing out.

Brakes are just as important to an automobile as an engine is. If cars could not be stopped easily, they would be too dangerous to ride in.

The brakes are large, rather flat steel cans. Each wheel fits on one of these cans. A garageman calls these cans the "brake drums." They go around as the wheel turns. Inside each drum are bands of a special material, mainly asbestos. When the driver "puts on the brake," these bands push against the inside rim of the brake drum and make the wheel slow down and stop. Hydraulic lines, which are thin pipes filled with oil, run between the brake pedal and the brake drums. When the driver steps on the brake pedal, pressure is put on the oil. The oil then pushes against the brake bands and forces them against the rims.

The last few years have seen power brakes and power steering come into wide use. In these improvements, electric motors help the driver do the work of stopping and turning the car. Air-conditioning units can now be put in most cars. Even telephones are available for automobiles. The manufacturing and servicing of automobiles and automobile equipment has grown to be one of the biggest industries in the United States. (See ENGINES, HEAT.)

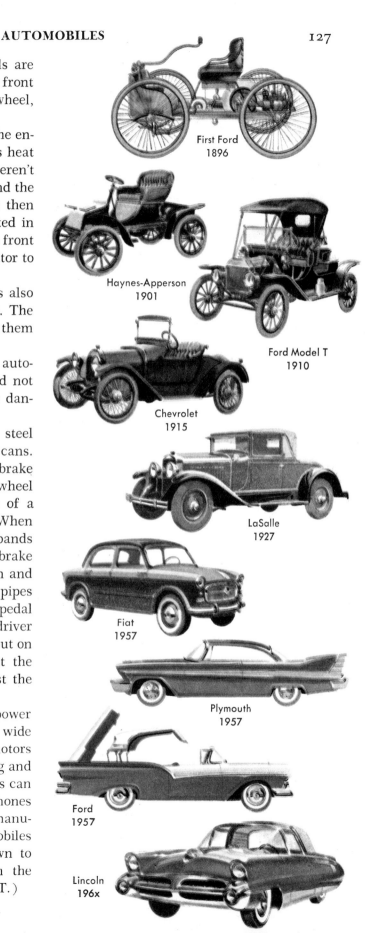

First Ford
1896

Haynes-Apperson
1901

Ford Model T
1910

Chevrolet
1915

LaSalle
1927

Fiat
1957

Plymouth
1957

Ford
1957

Lincoln
196x

AVALANCHE An avalanche is a snow-slide or a landslide. The snow or rocks come sliding down a steep slope. Most avalanches are near the tops of mountains. Slopes are likely to be very steep there.

Mountain climbing can be dangerous to the people who are doing the climbing. It can be dangerous, too, to the people down below, for a party of mountain climbers can easily start an avalanche. Even a mountain goat, by walking out on a snow field or a field of loose stones, can start one.

When a snowslide starts, it may make as much noise as a cannon. The snow may travel down the slope at a speed of 200 miles an hour. At the foot of the slope it may bury roads or railroads or even whole villages. Landslides are usually not so noisy when they start. But, if the land that is sliding is made up mostly of loose rocks, the rocks sometimes sound like a great pack of dogs as they come down. Landslides may bury roads and railroads and villages, just as snowslides sometimes do.

Snowslides happen most often in the spring, when the snow is beginning to melt. Landslides are most likely to come after heavy rains or during spring thaws.

The aye-aye loves tender bamboo shoots.

AYE-AYE (EYE-eye) The aye-aye is a furry animal about the size of a cat. It is one of the lemurs, relatives of the monkeys. Its name comes from the sounds it makes.

Not many people have ever seen an aye-aye. This little animal is found in only one small part of the world—the island of Madagascar—and it is not common even on this island. Besides, it comes out of hiding only at night.

Madagascar is near the east coast of Africa. Bamboo forests grow there. The aye-aye lives in these forests. It feeds on the soft inside part of the bamboo stems. It also eats grubs.

As the picture shows, an aye-aye has big eyes and big ears. Its bushy tail is as long as its body. The fingers on the aye-aye's hands are very long and bony. They are a big help in digging out grubs.

With its big eyes and long fingers, an aye-aye looks rather frightening at night. But the natives of Madagascar would not think of killing one of these small animals. They believe that a person who kills an aye-aye is sure to die within a year himself.

An avalanche can bury a train.

AZTECS About 300 years before Columbus made his first voyage to America, a tribe of Indians moved down from the north into what is now Mexico. These Indians were the Aztecs. They were hunters with bows and arrows.

At that time most of the Indians of Mexico were corngrowers. They had no weapons except clubs. It was easy for the Aztecs to conquer them. Two centuries after the Aztecs came, most of Mexico was under their rule.

The Aztecs chose an island in the middle of a lake as the place for their capital city. They named it Tenochtitlán (Tay noch tee TLAHN).

By the time Columbus sailed to the New World, Tenochtitlán was a large and beautiful city. Many of the buildings were made of light-colored stone that shone in the sunlight. There were great temples and beautiful homes. There was even a zoo. In the lake around the city were floating gardens. Canals in the city served as streets.

The Aztecs made jewelry of gold and silver. They made, for instance, ornaments for their lips and ears. They also wove fine cotton cloth and made beautiful vases. Their priests had wonderful robes and headdresses of feathers.

These Indians had no alphabet, but they could write. They wrote with pictures.

Twenty thousand captives were sacrificed on the steps of this temple.

Priest

Priest

Eagle
Warrior

Ambassador

High Priest

Their priests knew much about the stars and had worked out a calendar. One of the relics of the Aztecs is a great calendar stone that weighs more than 20 tons.

The Aztecs grew rapidly to be the most feared tribe in central Mexico. They forced many of the neighboring tribes to pay tribute to them. Those tribes or villages that refused to pay were attacked, and captives were taken away. The booty and the wealth which the Aztecs got from other tribes helped give Tenochtitlán the marvelous splendor that it had. Tenochtitlán grew from a small village of about 1,000 people in 1325 to a city of nearly 100,000 a couple of centuries later.

Religion was very important to the Aztecs. They worshiped gods of nature. Their chief god was a great sun god, and there were other gods of wind, light, rain, and fire. The Aztecs believed that their gods wanted human sacrifices.

In battle, the Aztecs did not try as hard to kill the enemy warriors as to capture them. Then the captives would be led off to a temple and offered up in sacrifice to the Aztec gods.

Soon after Columbus reached America, Spanish explorers rushed to the New World. One of them, Hernando Cortés, heard of the Aztecs and their wealthy ruler Montezuma II. He set out to conquer them.

Many of the Indian tribes who had long trembled before the Aztecs refused to help them in their battle with Cortés. Others joined forces with Cortés against the Aztecs. The Aztecs fought bravely, but they fought almost alone. The army of Cortés was better organized, and it had better weapons. The Aztecs were defeated. Their great ruler, Montezuma II, was killed. The beautiful city of Tenochtitlán fell to the Spaniards. Now Mexico City stands where this older city stood.

The Aztecs did not die out after they were conquered. Many of the Indians of Mexico today are descendants of the Aztecs of Montezuma's time. (See CORTES.)

Bb

The letter *B* began as the picture of a house. The picture was drawn in different ways (☐ ▱). Probably it was really a drawing of the yard around a house. The Egyptians used the picture in their writing. The makers of the first alphabet borrowed it for one of their letters.

The letter soon changed its shape (𝟿𝟿). As the Greeks used it, it changed still more (𝟹𝖡). When the Romans borrowed the alphabet from the Greeks, they made the letter like the capital *B* of today.

B has only one sound. In a few words it is silent.

BABYLONIA In western Asia there are two big rivers that flow southward into the Persian Gulf. They are the Tigris and the Euphrates. Before they reach the sea they run through a large, fertile plain. This plain came to be called Babylonia.

The region is now in the country of Iraq. It is sometimes called Mesopotamia. This name comes from the Greek words meaning "land between rivers." As the map shows, Mesopotamia is a part of a great "new moon" of rich land often spoken of as the Fertile Crescent.

Babylonia was one of the cradles of civilization. Much of what we have and do

today can be traced back to the peoples who lived there in ancient times. Writing, for instance, began there.

Some 5,000 years ago, while the rulers of Egypt were building their pyramids, the Sumerians lived in the Land of the Two Rivers. They had lived there for centuries. The Sumerians were builders, too. They had cities with good streets and with sewers. But they had no stone for building. They used brick instead. Some of the brick was sun dried; some was baked. Their buildings all crumbled away long ago.

These early people were good farmers. They drew water from the rivers to irri-

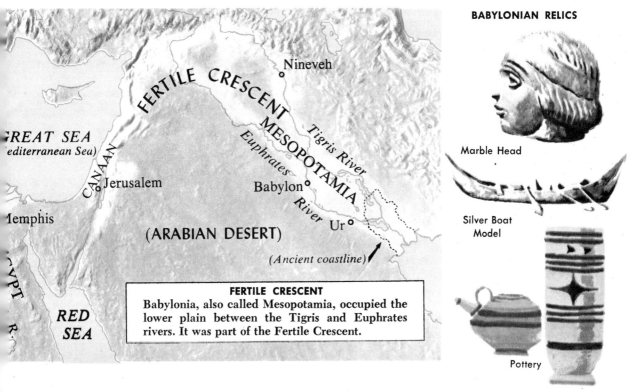

BABYLONIAN RELICS

Marble Head

Silver Boat Model

Pottery

FERTILE CRESCENT
Babylonia, also called Mesopotamia, occupied the lower plain between the Tigris and Euphrates rivers. It was part of the Fertile Crescent.

Nineveh

GREAT SEA
(Mediterranean Sea)

CANAAN

Jerusalem

Memphis

EGYPT R.

RED SEA

FERTILE CRESCENT

MESOPOTAMIA

Tigris River

Euphrates

Babylon

River

Ur

(ARABIAN DESERT)

(Ancient coastline)

Tiglath-pileser III, an Assyrian King

copper tools. The children had toys to play with, just as American children have. There were whistles, rattles, wagons, and toy animals on wheels.

The Sumerians could write. They wrote with pointed sticks on soft clay tablets. The sticks made wedge-shaped marks in the clay. Writing done in this way is called cuneiform (ku NE i form). "Cuneiform" means "wedge-shaped." This writing was used mostly for keeping records of such things as the sale of land and livestock.

The Sumerians also knew a great deal about using numbers, but often they counted by sixties rather than by hundreds as we do. The 60 seconds in a minute and the 60 minutes in an hour can be traced back to this old way of counting.

From time to time tribes from the desert round about forced their way into the Land of the Two Rivers. About 3,700 years ago a leader from one of these tribes became the ruler of the land. His name was Hammurabi. Hammurabi turned out to be a wise ruler. For one thing, he had the laws of the land gathered together and carved on a great stone tablet. They were written in cuneiform. The tablet can still be read.

There were 282 laws in the Code of Hammurabi. Some of the laws seem rather harsh to us now, but on the whole they were just. They helped protect the common

gate their farms. They dug big canals to carry the water. On their farms they raised barley and wheat. They had oxen to help them plow their fields.

On their canals and rivers the Sumerians used boats. For travel and carrying loads on land they used carts and chariots. They had donkeys to pull the carts and chariots; perhaps they also had horses.

Razors and toilet kits and cosmetics we think of as being modern, but these people of long ago had them. They also had beautiful jewelry of gold and silver, and good

An Alabaster Carving of a King Hunting Lions

Here were located the famous Hanging Gardens mentioned in the Bible. These were one of the Seven Wonders of the Ancient World.

The Palace of Nebuchadnezzar at Babylon

people. Here are a few of them:

"If a man cut down a tree in a man's orchard without the consent of the owner of the orchard, he shall pay one-half mina of silver.

"If a man hire an ox or an ass and a lion kill it on the plain, the loss is the owner's affair.

"If a man hire an ox and cause its death through neglect or abuse, he shall restore ox for ox to the owner of the ox.

"If a builder erect a house for a man and do not make its construction firm, and the house which he built collapse and cause the death of the owner, that builder shall be put to death.

"If the son of a gentleman smite the son of a gentleman of his own rank on the cheek, he shall pay one mina of silver.

"If either an officer or a constable who is ordered to go on an errand of the King do not go, or if he hire a substitute, that officer or constable shall be put to death. His hired substitute shall take to himself his house."

Hammurabi made the city of Babylon his capital. His people were called Babylonians. Under him the Babylonians be-

came great traders. They sent caravans far and wide on trading expeditions. In their trading they used lumps of silver as money. Bills for the goods were written in cuneiform. So were all sorts of business papers. Many of these had envelopes of clay around them. Every businessman had a seal—a little cylinder of stone with a picture carved on it. He signed a paper by rolling his seal across the wet clay. Envelopes were marked in the same way. Some of the seals were true works of art.

The Babylonians built buildings of brick, just as the earlier people in the Land of

A Market Place Inside the City Walls of Babylon

the Two Rivers had done. Their buildings did not last, but we know that the builders used arches.

After Hammurabi, a people from the mountains to the north, the Kassites, poured into Babylonia. They used horses in their fighting. The invaders did not bring many new ideas. They learned and followed the Babylonian ways of living.

Long before Hammurabi's time a little kingdom had grown up to the north on the Tigris. It was Assur. Several hundred years after Hammurabi the people of Assur, who were called the Assyrians, conquered Babylonia and much land round about. They built up a strong empire.

The Assyrians were fighters. Their big armies had weapons of iron. They had war chariots drawn by horses. They had battering rams, too. These were useful in knocking down the walls of cities.

The Assyrians were also great builders. Their capital was not Babylon. Instead it was Nineveh (NIN e veh), which was to the north of Babylon. The walls of Nineveh stretched for more than three miles along the Tigris. Within the walls there were many beautiful buildings. They were decorated with sculptures, some of which we can still see.

The earliest library anyone knows about was built up by an emperor of Assyria. More than 20,000 clay tablets have been found in the ruins of this library.

In spite of their strong armies, the Assyrians could not hold their empire. Babylonia was conquered by a desert tribe, the Chaldeans (kal DEE ans).

The greatest Chaldean ruler was Nebuchadnezzar II. Babylon was again the capital. Nebuchadnezzar built high walls with gardens at the top around the city and around the palaces. The walls and gardens were one of the Seven Wonders of the Ancient World.

The sun, moon, and stars played a part in the religions of the Chaldeans. The priests learned a great deal about these heavenly bodies. We now have seven days in a week because the Chaldeans had in each week one day to honor the sun, one day to honor the moon, and a day to honor each of the five planets they knew about.

While Nebuchadnezzar was rebuilding his wonderful city of Babylon, a strong empire was growing up in the east. It was Persia. Soon the Persian Empire swallowed up the Land of the Two Rivers. For centuries from then on it was only a small part of one great empire after another. (See IRAQ; LIBRARIES; NUMBERS; SEVEN WONDERS OF THE WORLD; WRITING.)

Tiles from the Ishtar Gate

BACH, JOHANN SEBASTIAN (1685-1750) Music as we know it today began with Johann Sebastian Bach. He ranks as one of the world's greatest composers. Most of his music was written to be played or sung in churches.

Bach was born in Eisenach, Germany. From early childhood he was interested in music. Many of his relatives were musical. Once each year the Bachs held what they called "family day." For the whole day they all sang, danced, and played instruments.

Before Johann was ten years old his parents died, and he went to live with an older brother. This brother taught him to play the clavichord, an instrument much like a piano. Once his brother refused to let him use a big book of difficult music. Johann then took the book secretly and copied all the music by moonlight. The strain on his eyes may help account for his blindness towards the end of his life.

Bach began to earn his living when he was 15. He sang in a church choir. Before long he was given a position as organist. He became the greatest organist who had ever lived.

Dukes and princes knew and admired Bach. But he lived simply. He had many children—20 in all—and enjoyed being with them.

In Bach's time he was famous as an organist, not as a composer. It took a hundred years for people to discover from his music what a great genius he was. (See COMPOSERS; MUSIC.)

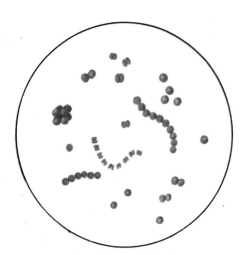

Round Bacteria (Cocci)

A flea is as big as millions of bacteria together.

BACTERIA (bak TEER i a) The tiniest plants we know about are much too small to be seen without a microscope. These tiny plants are called bacteria. Inside this letter O there would be room for thousands of bacteria. These little plants are almost colorless.

Bacteria are nearly everywhere. They are in the food we eat, in the water we drink, and in the air we breathe. They are in the ground we walk on. They are even inside us. They grow best where it is warm, dark, and damp.

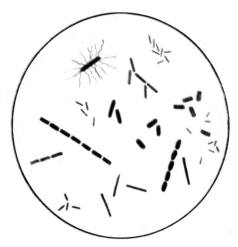

Rod-shaped Bacteria (Bacilli)

There are more than a thousand different kinds of bacteria. They can all be sorted into three shapes. Some are round. Others are rod-shaped. Still others are twisted, or spiral. They may have tiny "hairs" that help them to swim about in water and in other liquids.

Bacteria never die of old age. As soon as one grows to its full size, it divides into two bacteria. It may take only 20 minutes for one of these tiny plants to grow up and then divide.

Some bacteria are disease germs. Some make our teeth decay. Some spoil food.

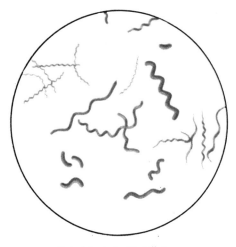

Spiral Bacteria (Spirilla)

But many kinds of bacteria are helpful. Some take nitrogen from the air and put it into soil. Green plants can then use it. Some help make vinegar and cheese. More important, some bacteria make dead plants and animals decay. Without bacteria to cause decay, the earth would soon have no room for living things. (See DISEASE GERMS.)

BACTERIOLOGY The study of bacteria is called bacteriology. It is one of the more modern sciences.

Bacteria were first seen through a microscope nearly 300 years ago, but no one knew they were important until 200 years later. Then scientists began to find out how much these tiny plants help and harm us. After that the science of bacteriology grew fast. From the first most bacteriologists have been chiefly interested in the bacteria that cause disease.

In the beginning scientists had trouble raising only the kinds of bacteria they were interested in studying. Other kinds grew right along with the wanted kinds. It was hard to shut out these unwanted bacteria. But finally scientists learned how, and now they raise just the kinds they wish to study. (See PASTEUR.)

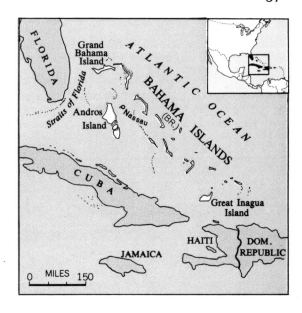

BAGPIPE No other musical instrument looks or sounds like a bagpipe. When it is played, a queer drone serves as a background for the tune. The bagpipe gets its name because a bag filled with air furnishes air for the pipes that make the sound.

The bagpipe is a very old instrument. The ancient Egyptians, Greeks, and Romans all had it. Today the bagpipe is thought of as the instrument of the Scotch Highlanders.

A Highland bagpipe has five tubes. The player blows into the bag through one. He plays the tune on another. The other three tubes make the droning sound.

BAHAMAS The first land that Columbus saw in the New World was a small island. He named it San Salvador. This little island is in the group called the Bahamas. The Bahamas are not far from Florida. The nearest is less than 100 miles away.

There are more than 700 islands in the group. All of them are small. They rise only a little way above the sea. On many of them there are no people at all.

The soil is poor. It is made up mostly of broken shells and coral. The islands get much rain in the winter and some during the rest of the year. But the rain sinks fast through the porous soil and leaves it dry. There is not a single river in the Bahamas.

Even on the poor soil some crops are raised. Pineapples, tomatoes, and sisal are among them. Some natives fish for sponges. Some make salt from sea water. Others make straw hats. But most of the people depend on tourists for a living. The Bahamas are a pleasant vacation spot, and many people go there to bathe, sail, and fish.

The islands, although they are close to the United States, belong to Britain. They have a British governor. He lives in a beautiful palace in Nassau, the capital.

The Bahamas are in the path of hurricanes. Once in a while a hurricane does great damage to these islands.

Cooper Hawk

The chief food of this kind of deer is a kind of wild rose. The deer in turn are eaten by mountain lions. If they are let alone, the number of mule deer, mountain lions, and roses does not change much.

But suppose for some reason the number of mule deer should suddenly increase. Soon the number of mountain lions would increase, because there would be so much food for them. At the same time, roses for the mule deer to eat would become scarce. The number of mule deer would soon be back to normal again.

The United States government once decided to protect the mule deer by shooting all the mountain lions in the region. There were soon so many deer that they ate up all

the wild roses. They began eating young trees and sagebrush. There still was not enough food for them, and many died of starvation. The government learned a lesson. In the National Parks great care is now taken not to upset the balance in nature.

BALANCE IN NATURE Not very many years ago the farmers in one county of an eastern state began to complain about hawks. The hawks were carrying off their chickens. County officials decided to help the farmers by paying people to kill the hawks. Many were killed—so many that the farmers no longer complained that the hawks were catching their chickens. But now they complained about something else. Field mice were eating up their grain.

No one had stopped to think that hawks eat field mice. They eat many more field mice than chickens. With fewer hawks to eat them, there came to be more and more field mice. Killing the hawks had upset what scientists call the "balance in nature."

What scientists mean by balance in nature is this: Every region has its plants and animals. If nothing unusual happens, the number of each kind of plant and animal stays about the same.

To understand how balance in nature is brought about in a region, we must know about the food habits of the animals of the region. In one part of southwestern United States, for instance, there are mule deer.

Field Mice

People cannot keep from upsetting the balance in nature somewhat. We cannot build big cities or plow new land for crops or drain swamps without disturbing many wild plants and animals. But often we disturb the balance for no good reason. Killing off some kind of plant or animal is a common way. Taking a plant or animal into a new region is another way of disturbing this balance in nature.

Some of the early settlers in Australia took the prickly-pear cactus there. They thought that it would make a pretty house plant. They took the jackrabbit to Australia, too. In this new home rabbits and prickly-pear cactus plants had no enemies. Soon there were so many rabbits and so many cactus plants that they both were terrible nuisances. The government of Australia has spent large sums of money trying to get rid of them.

People are not always to blame when the balance in nature is upset. Every once in a while unusual weather makes some kind of animal multiply so fast that we say there is a plague of it. There have been, for instance, many plagues of grasshoppers. But sooner or later, if people do not make any blunders, such a plague ends. The region comes back into balance again.

Mountain Lion

Wild Roses

Mule Deer

Balboa claimed the Pacific for Spain.

BALBOA, VASCO NÚÑEZ DE (1475-1517)

Many explorers and adventurers rushed to the New World after the voyages of Columbus. One was Balboa, born a Spanish gentleman.

Hoping to make his fortune, Balboa sailed for America in 1501 with another Spanish explorer. He first tried his hand at farming on the island of Hispaniola in the Caribbean, but he was not successful.

Some years later, to escape his debts, he hid on a ship bound for the mainland. He finally reached Darien, now called Panama, and became governor there. Balboa conquered the Indians round about, but he treated them so well that they were friendly. From some of the Indian chiefs he heard of a great sea that lay beyond the mountains.

On September 1, 1513, Balboa set out to find this great sea. With him he took 190 Spaniards and 1,000 Indians. They had to hack through deep jungle. The going was always hard. At last, on September 25, Balboa climbed to the top of a bare hill and saw a vast sea in the distance. He named it the Southern Sea. It was, of course, the Pacific Ocean. Balboa was the first white man to see it from the New World.

Four days later Balboa reached the shore and waded out into the ocean with his sword held high. He claimed the sea and all the lands that bordered it for Spain. But he got no reward. Four years later he was put to death by a new Spanish governor. (See EXPLORERS; PACIFIC OCEAN.)

BALLET

There are different ways of telling a story. It can be told in words. It can be told in pictures. It can be told in music. It can be acted out. Or it can be told by still another way — by dancing. Dancing that tells a story is called a ballet.

The dancing in a ballet is done to music, but the story is told by the movements of the dancers. There is no singing or speaking.

The dancers in the picture at the right are telling the story of *Sleeping Beauty*. The music for this famous ballet was written by the Russian composer Tschaikowsky (chy KOFF ski). The movements of its dancers were worked out by the French ballet master Petipa.

A ballet is a work of art just as a beautiful picture is. The person who plans a ballet is an artist. So is each dancer.

Sometimes ballet is called toe dancing. It is true that in some ballets the dancers do dance on their toes. But a great deal of the dancing in ballets is not toe dancing. Toe dancing is used to give the idea of lightness and airiness. It is never put into a ballet unless it fits the story.

Back in the days of ancient Greece and Rome there were dances that told stories of the gods. Even longer ago in Egypt there were dances that told stories of the planets. But the ballet of today had its beginnings about 600 years ago. It began as a kind of entertainment in the courts of the rulers of

1st Position   2nd Position   3rd Position   4th Position

The Sleeping Beauty ballet tells a story in dance.

Italy. Two hundred years later ballet was popular in the French court. The French king Louis XIV founded a ballet school.

On a ballet program today there are often some French words. The names of many ballets are French. But there may be other French words, too. A part of a ballet that is danced by just two people is called a *pas de deux* (pa de DOO). Such French words remind us that France was once the leader in ballet.

Later the rulers of Russia became interested in ballet. They offered a great deal of money to the best ballet masters and dancers of France. They founded a ballet school. Soon Russia was the leader in ballet.

Today there are many ballet companies. All opera companies, too, have ballet dancers, for ballets are a part of many operas. No one country now leads in ballet.

Ballet is not easy to learn. A boy or girl who wishes to be a ballet dancer has to begin going to a ballet school very early. Some begin when they are only three or four. All the parts in a ballet used to be danced by men. But now a girl has as good a chance as a boy of being a famous ballet dancer. (See ARTS; MUSIC; OPERA.)

5th Position
Croise
Arabesque
Attitude
Entrechat
Bâttement a la Seconde
Grand Jeté
Passé

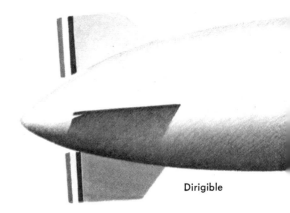

Dirigible

BALLOONS On September 19, 1783, there was great excitement at Versailles in France. The Montgolfier brothers were going to try to send a balloon up into the sky. They had tried a balloon a few months before, and it had worked. Now they were going to try again before the King. And this time the balloon was to have passengers—a rooster, a sheep, and a duck were to ride in a basket hanging from the balloon.

The balloon was made of linen and was open at the bottom. Ropes held it in place over a fire of straw. A mixture of smoke and hot air rose from the fire into the balloon. The mixture was lighter than the cool air round about.

The ropes were loosened, and the balloon rose. Up and up it went. When the smoke and hot air cooled, the balloon came down.

Soon there were balloons that could carry people. Many of these balloons were filled with hydrogen, the lightest gas known.

The first balloons were at the mercy of the wind. The passengers could not guide them. But they could make them go up or down. They carried bags of sand or something else heavy for ballast. To go higher, they threw ballast overboard. To come down, they let some gas out of the bag.

About 60 years ago the first dirigibles were built. By means of engines, propellers, and rudders they could be made to go in any direction. Some of the later dirigibles had a framework of aluminum. These were called zeppelins in honor of Count Ferdinand von Zeppelin, who invented them. In 1929 a zeppelin flew all the way around the

One of the First Passenger Balloons

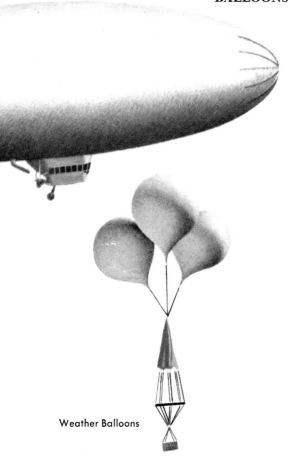

Weather Balloons

BALTIC SEA Norway and Sweden are on a long peninsula that reaches south from the northernmost coast of Europe. To the east of this long peninsula is the Baltic Sea.

Six countries touch the Baltic Sea. They are Sweden, Finland, the Soviet Union, Poland, Germany, and Denmark. Three of their capitals are seaports on the shores of the Baltic. They are Copenhagen, the capital of Denmark, Stockholm, the capital of Sweden, and Helsinki, the capital of Finland. Helsinki is on an arm of the Baltic called the Gulf of Finland. Russia's biggest seaport, Leningrad, is also on this gulf.

As anyone would guess, the Baltic Sea is a busy place. Boats travel back and forth among the countries that touch it. Big ships from faraway lands come in from the Atlantic Ocean and the North Sea to its ports, too. To get from the North Sea to the Baltic, ships used to have to travel around Denmark. Now they can take a short cut through the Kiel Canal, which crosses Germany just south of Denmark.

The Baltic would be even busier than it is if its water were saltier. It has so little salt in it that it freezes easily. For three or four months every winter most of its ports are icebound.

world. But in 1937 a terrible accident put a stop to travel in zeppelins. A big zeppelin, the "Hindenburg," burned up just as it finished a flight from Germany to the United States. A spark had set fire to the hydrogen in its bag.

Helium is a gas that will not burn. It is not as light as hydrogen, but it is much safer. The balloons of today, if they carry people, are filled with helium.

Airplanes are now so fast and safe that people no longer think of traveling by balloon. But balloons are still used. They are most useful in helping to explore the upper atmosphere. They carry cameras and other scientific instruments high into the air. Weathermen use balloons to help chart the winds. And in 1957 a big balloon carried an American airman, Major David G. Simons, 19 miles above the surface of the earth to the greatest height yet reached by man.

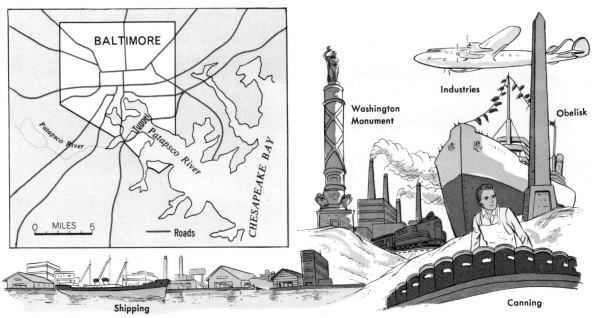

BALTIMORE Ocean shipping helped Baltimore grow to be the sixth-largest city in the United States. Baltimore handles twice as much cargo as Boston, and almost as much as Philadelphia. It is the largest city in Maryland. In fact, almost half of the people of the entire state live there.

Two towns called Baltimore were started during the 1600's, but neither one lasted. The present Baltimore was founded in 1729. Like the two earlier Baltimores, it took its name from Lord Baltimore of England, the founder of Maryland.

Baltimore is on the Patapsco River. Ships can sail down this river into Chesapeake Bay and then into the Atlantic Ocean. In the city's earliest days ships began carrying to Europe grain and tobacco from the rich farmlands around Chesapeake Bay. On the return trip they brought in manufactured goods that were sold to Southern planters. Some of the ships themselves were built in Baltimore.

In 1904 a violent fire destroyed much of Baltimore. The new city built on the ashes of the old one was much better in some ways. Streets were widened, and bigger buildings were put up. Baltimore began to attract manufacturers. Today the city has steel mills and factories that manufacture chemicals, machinery, airplanes, fertilizer, and clothing.

Baltimore still has its monument to George Washington, the first to be erected to him. "The Star Spangled Banner" was written in Baltimore after the British shelled Fort McHenry during the War of 1812. (See MARYLAND.)

Bamboo is the world's tallest grass.

BAMBOO The grass family is a very large and important plant family. Most of our grains belong to it. In the grass family there is one tree, the bamboo. A bamboo tree may be 100 feet tall with a trunk a foot across. But, as a rule, bamboo trees are rather small. The trunk is jointed like a cornstalk. Like most grass stems, it is hollow.

Bamboo trees grow in warm, moist lands. They are common in some parts of Asia and on many islands in the Pacific.

Bamboo seeds are good to eat. But bamboo trees do not bear seeds every year. Some bear seeds only once every 60 years.

The seeds are not the only part of the bamboo that can be eaten. Young bamboo shoots, or sprouts, are used as food, too. They are often used in chop suey.

The leaves of the bamboo make good food for cattle. They are also used in making paper. The hard, hollow trunks are useful in building houses and bridges, and in making furniture, curtains, and baskets. Small ones make good fishing poles. Large ones serve as water pipes.

BANANA Month in and month out bananas can be bought in our fruit stores. But until about a hundred years ago few people outside the hot, wet lands where this fruit grows had ever tasted a banana. Bananas spoil quickly. They could not be shipped to other lands until there were fast boats to carry them and ways of keeping them cold on their journey.

Our bananas come to us mostly from Central America, the West Indies, and Hawaii. They are picked green, and are handled carefully so that they will not be bruised. After they reach the market, they are sometimes ripened with chemicals.

Bananas grow on tall plants that are often called trees. They are not real trees, because they have no woody trunks. The trunk of a banana plant is a sort of tube made up of the lower parts of the plant's huge leaves. Yellowish flowers blossom at the top of a stem that grows up through the center of the tube of leaves. A bunch of bananas develops from the cluster of flowers. A banana plant produces only one bunch of bananas in its lifetime.

Not all bananas are like those in fruit stores. In Africa bananas grow that are two feet long and as big around as a man's arm. They have to be cooked to be good to eat.

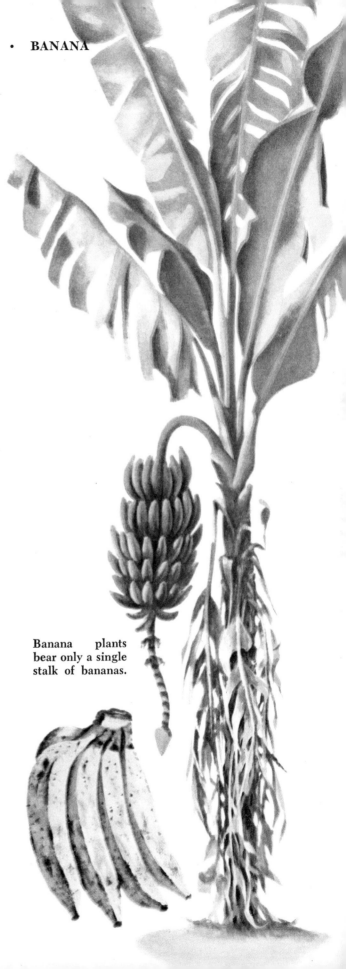

Banana plants bear only a single stalk of bananas.

Many instruments are in a modern band.

BAND Seven hundred years ago little bands of musicians wandered from town to town in Europe. Their instruments were all wind and percussion instruments. These were not as easily damaged by bad weather as stringed instruments. Besides, the music from them could be heard for a much greater distance. Since most of the instruments were brass, the early bands were called brass bands.

Five centuries later military bands were formed in Europe. Ancient armies had

Brasses are long, bent tubes of brass.

men who used trumpets and other wind instruments to give signals to the troops. But there had never been any real military bands before. Today nearly every military camp has its band.

Military bands use not only brass wind instruments but woodwinds, too. They also use the saxophone, an instrument that had not been invented in the days of the first brass bands.

Military bands lead troops in marching. They are therefore sometimes called marching bands.

Today there are many marching bands besides military bands. Almost every college and high school has one. Many towns have marching bands, too. In a big parade we expect to see and hear several bands.

Some marching bands do clever marching routines. The players pride themselves on their uniforms. Usually the bands are led by gaily dressed drum majors with whirling batons.

Now there are concert bands, too. In concert bands, in addition to the wind and per-

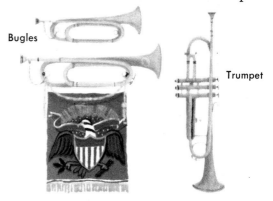

Bugles

Trumpet

Modern trumpets are much like ancient bugles.

cussion instruments, one or two harps and double basses may be used.

For many years John Philip Sousa was America's outstanding band leader. He earned the nickname of "March King" because he wrote so many marches for bands to play. One of the best known is "The Stars and Stripes Forever." (See PERCUSSION INSTRUMENTS; WIND INSTRUMENTS.)

Bandicoots are small cousins of kangaroos.

BANDICOOT The bandicoot in the picture lives in Australia and on nearby islands. The name "bandicoot" means "pig rat." But Australian bandicoots are neither pigs nor rats. Probably they got their name because they look like the bandicoot of India, which *is* a rat.

Some Australian bandicoots are the size of big rabbits, but others are less than a foot long. Like their relatives the kangaroos, they carry their babies in pouches.

The bandicoots of Australia come to gardens at dusk to find food—plants and mice and insects. They are very energetic. There is a saying that whenever a bandicoot is awake it is busy. Bandicoots were once far more common than they are now.

BANKS AND BANKING Mr. Smith is buying a new car. It costs $3,000. Mr. Smith does not have $3,000 with him. He writes out an order to his bank to pay the car dealer the $3,000. An order of this kind is called a check.

Many people put their money in a bank; they carry blank checks which they can make out to anyone they please. Carrying a check is far safer than carrying money. If money is lost or stolen there is little chance of getting it back. If a blank check is lost, no harm is done. If a check that has been made out is lost or stolen, the bank can be told not to cash it. Checks make it simple to send money to other parts of the country, too. A check can easily be mailed.

The car dealer does not actually have to go to Mr. Smith's bank to cash Mr. Smith's check. He merely takes the check to his own bank. His bank then gets the money from Mr. Smith's bank.

A person who puts money in a bank and then pays it out with checks has what is called a checking account. A person may also have a savings account. People put money in savings accounts when they plan to leave the money in the bank for quite a long time. They have to go or write to the bank to take money out when they want it. Most banks pay a small amount for the use of the money left with them in savings accounts. This is called interest.

Banks also lend money. Suppose Mr. Brown wants to build a new factory or buy a farm. He has some money, but not enough. He goes to his bank. If the men who run the bank feel sure that Mr. Brown will be able to pay the money back, they lend it to him. They charge him a small amount of money for the use of the money that they lend him. This charge is also called interest.

Many banks have safe-deposit vaults. Here people may keep such things as jew-

A customer explains why he needs a loan.

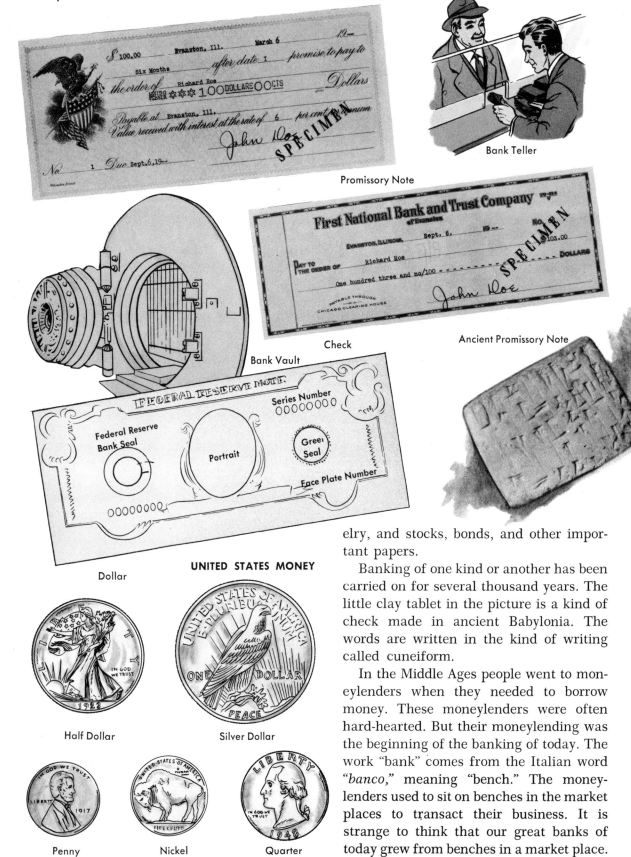

Promissory Note

Bank Teller

Bank Vault

Check

Ancient Promissory Note

Federal Reserve Bank Seal

Portrait

Series Number

Green Seal

Face Plate Number

UNITED STATES MONEY

Dollar

Half Dollar

Silver Dollar

Penny

Nickel

Quarter

elry, and stocks, bonds, and other important papers.

Banking of one kind or another has been carried on for several thousand years. The little clay tablet in the picture is a kind of check made in ancient Babylonia. The words are written in the kind of writing called cuneiform.

In the Middle Ages people went to moneylenders when they needed to borrow money. These moneylenders were often hard-hearted. But their moneylending was the beginning of the banking of today. The work "bank" comes from the Italian word "banco," meaning "bench." The moneylenders used to sit on benches in the market places to transact their business. It is strange to think that our great banks of today grew from benches in a market place.

BANYAN One banyan tree may look like a whole grove of trees, for a banyan has many trunks. A single tree may have more than a thousand.

The banyan is found in southern Asia and other tropical lands. It belongs to the same family as the fig and the mulberry.

As a rule, a banyan tree begins its life in the top of another tree. The banyan has bright red fruits that look like cherries. Birds and monkeys and fruit bats eat them. One of these animals may leave the seed of a fruit in the top of a palm tree. The seed sprouts. The baby tree sends a root down into the ground. Soon more roots grow down around the palm tree. The little banyan branches out fast.

At last the palm tree dies and rots away. But by this time the banyan does not need the palm tree to hold it up.

As the banyan keeps on growing, roots grow down from its branches. They prop up the branches and carry water and minerals to the leaves. They grow to be trunks. The trunks of a big banyan tree in India were once measured. The biggest trunk was 13 feet across. There were 230 trunks between 2 and 3 feet across. There were 3,000 smaller trunks. Seven thousand people could stand under this one tree.

Each branch of a banyan tree has its own trunk.

Sycamore Bark   Hickory Bark

BARK Every tree has its own kind of bark. The bark of a paper birch is smooth and white. The bark of a hickory tree is dark and shaggy. The bark of a sycamore has patches of brown and white. But bark, no matter how it looks, always helps a tree in the same ways.

The outer layer of bark is made of cork, which is waterproof. This layer is a protection against injury from animals and against drying winds. The inner layer of bark can be hurt easily and needs protection. It plays an important part in the life of the tree, for it is made up partly of tubes, called "sieve tubes," that carry food for the tree. Just inside the bark is another region that needs protection. It is the region where new wood is formed. In the new wood water travels up from the roots to the treetop.

Once in a while lightning strikes a tree and peels off all its bark. The tree then has no chance at all of living.

The Indians used to make canoes of birchbark. Bark can be used in building other things, too. Several drugs come from bark. One of them is quinine. The spice cinnamon comes from the bark of the cinnamon tree. Tannin used in making leather comes from the bark of oak trees. Cork comes from the bark of the cork oak. Bark helps people as well as the trees it grows on. (See TREES.)

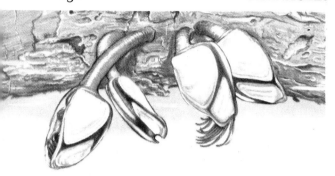

BARNACLES Anyone who goes to the seashore is likely to see many of the little animals called barnacles. Barnacles are found on rocks along the seashore. They are found, too, on floating logs, on piers, on the bottoms of ships, and even on other animals. Seashells picked up on the shore may have tiny barnacle shells fastened to them.

Barnacles are cousins of the lobsters and the crabs, but they do not look much like these cousins of theirs. The barnacles that grow on rocks look like tiny volcanoes. Those that grow on ships have stalks. They are often called goose barnacles.

Barnacles may be crowded closely together. More than 2,000 have been found growing on a rock in a space no bigger than this page. So many may grow on the bottom of a ship that they have to be cleaned off.

Baby barnacles swim about freely. But soon they fasten themselves to something solid and grow a shell. Barnacles stay for the rest of their lives in the place where they settle.

A barnacle never leaves its shell. It never even sticks its head out. But it does put its feathery feet out through the opening in its shell. These feet kick tiny plants and animals into its mouth. When a barnacle is not covered with water, it pulls in its feet and closes its shell. (See CRUSTACEANS.)

BARNUM, PHINEAS TAYLOR (1810-1891) Everyone who loves a circus should be grateful to P. T. Barnum. He did much to make the circus into the wonderful show it is now.

Long before he started a circus Barnum put on shows that were like today's circus sideshows. Many of his early shows were hoaxes. A hoax is something that is meant to fool people. One of Barnum's hoaxes was the "Fejee Mermaid." The "mermaid" was nothing but the stuffed head and shoulders of a monkey sewed to the tail of a fish.

The Siamese twins were one of his exhibits that was not a hoax. The big elephant Jumbo was another. Probably his most famous show was a group of dwarfs. He named one of them "General" Tom Thumb. On a tour to Europe he even presented Tom Thumb to Queen Victoria.

This great showman persuaded the famous singer called "the Swedish Nightingale" to come to sing in the United States. Her real name was Jenny Lind.

When Barnum was nearly 60 he put many of his shows together to make a circus. He called it "The Greatest Show on Earth." James A. Bailey was another circus owner. In a few years Barnum and Bailey made their circuses into one.

Barnum used big parades and brass bands to advertise. He made a great day of the day the circus came to town. (See CIRCUS.)

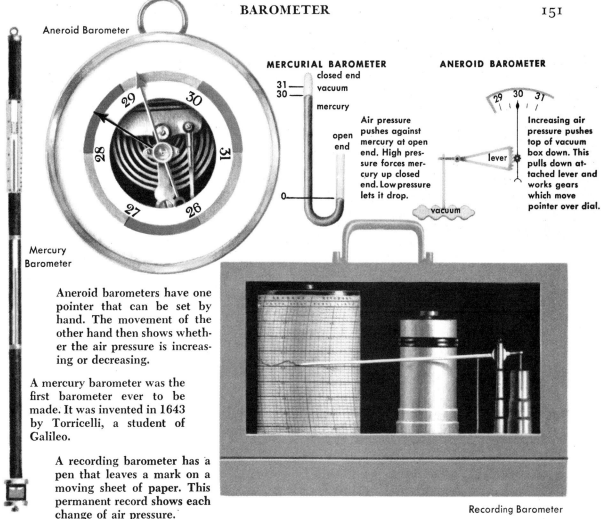

Aneroid Barometer

Mercury Barometer

MERCURIAL BAROMETER

closed end
vacuum
mercury
open end
31
30
0

Air pressure pushes against mercury at open end. High pressure forces mercury up closed end. Low pressure lets it drop.

ANEROID BAROMETER

29 30 31

lever

vacuum

Increasing air pressure pushes top of vacuum box down. This pulls down attached lever and works gears which move pointer over dial.

Aneroid barometers have one pointer that can be set by hand. The movement of the other hand then shows whether the air pressure is increasing or decreasing.

A mercury barometer was the first barometer ever to be made. It was invented in 1643 by Torricelli, a student of Galileo.

A recording barometer has a pen that leaves a mark on a moving sheet of paper. This permanent record shows each change of air pressure.

Recording Barometer

BAROMETER A bucketful of air weighs only a little. But our ocean of air is so deep that it pushes on everything on the earth with a great deal of force. Barometers measure this force.

In some places the air pushes harder than in other places. At the top of a mountain, for instance, it does not push so hard as in the valleys near by. There is not so much air above to press down. The air pressure, we say, is less on the mountaintop. Even in the same place, the air pressure does not stay the same day after day. It changes with the weather.

Because barometers can measure changes in air pressure, they are very useful to the weatherman. They help him predict the weather. They are very useful to airplane pilots, too. They help tell how high

a plane is above sea level. They help mountain climbers in the same way.

There are different kinds of barometers, as the pictures at the top of the page show. The different kinds do not look much alike.

In some barometers there is a tube which has mercury in it. Mercury barometers look a little like big thermometers.

In other barometers there are one or more little boxes with a partial vacuum inside. Barometers of this kind are called aneroid barometers. An aneroid barometer has a hand that moves whenever the air pressure changes.

Some barometers keep a record of the air pressure. A pen on the hand of the barometer makes a mark on a moving sheet of paper. (See AIR; GUERICKE, OTTO VON; VACUUM; WEATHER.)

Get out of the water if barracuda come near!

Pacific Barracuda

Great Barracuda

BARRACUDA There are several kinds of barracudas, all salt-water fishes. The largest of them is the great barracuda. It is found in the ocean near Florida. All the barracudas are fierce, but the great barracuda is especially so. It is sometimes called the tiger of the sea. This big fish—it may be eight or nine feet long—even attacks people. Its teeth are as sharp as knives. Sharks are often blamed for wounds really made by the great barracuda.

Barracudas usually lie in hiding, ready to dart out swiftly after their prey. They will leap high out of the water in their efforts to catch flying fish.

The barracudas are good game fishes. They fight ferociously when caught. They tire quickly, but a fisherman has a right to boast if he lands a big one.

BARTER An old Egyptian picture shows a man trading an ox for five measures of meal, eleven measures of oil, and a mat. The diary of an early settler in Illinois reports that he traded 80 acres of land for a shotgun and a yoke of oxen. The Pygmies of Africa bring fruit to the edge of the forest land where they live and trade it for meat. Trading in this way—trading without the use of money—is called barter.

Barter was used before money was invented. It is still a common way of trading today. Some savage tribes do not yet have money, and even in civilized countries much trading still goes on without the use of money.

But trading without money is not always easy. An explorer once wanted to buy a boat for a trip up a river in Africa. He found a native who had a boat to trade, but the native wanted to trade it for ivory. The explorer had no ivory. He could get ivory from another native in exchange for cloth, but he had no cloth. At last the explorer found a third native who had some cloth he was willing to trade for wire. The explorer did have some wire. He traded the wire for the cloth, the cloth for the ivory, and the ivory for the boat. In barter there is always the problem of finding someone who is willing to give up what he has for what is being offered. A visitor in Borneo watched a native wandering about a market place for days with a big lump of beeswax. No one who had anything this native wanted, wanted beeswax.

Barter is made harder by the fact that some things cannot be divided without being spoiled. A diver who has found a good pearl may need food, but the pearl is worth much more food than he needs at one time.

ITEMS OF BARTER

Feathers

Beads

Breadfruit

Tiger Teeth

Spanish explorers gave the Florida Indians beads in exchange for food.

He cannot trade a small piece of the pearl for a small amount of food, for the pearl is ruined if it is broken.

Another difficulty with barter is that a great deal of time often has to be spent in bargaining. Suppose a native who has bananas to trade bargains with a native who has nuts to trade. They decide that six bananas for a handful of nuts is a fair trade. If the man with bananas then wants to trade for dried herbs, the bargaining has to begin all over again.

Wages would be a real problem if we had to go back to barter. How, for example, would the owner of an automobile factory pay his workmen? Automobiles are the only things his factory makes. He might give each workman an automobile at the end of his first six months. A workman might be glad to have the automobile. But

he would not always want to be paid in automobiles. He would want something he could divide among the milkman, grocer, butcher, and shoemaker.

An opera singer once gave a concert on an island in the South Pacific where barter was a common way of trading. She was to be given a third of everything that was taken in at the concert. Her share turned out to be 3 pigs, 23 turkeys, 44 chickens, 5,000 coconuts, and hundreds of bananas, lemons, and oranges. She could not sell her share for money, for there was no money on the island. She certainly could not eat it all, and she could not carry it all away with her. In the end she fed most of the fruit to the pigs, turkeys, and chickens, and then gave them away. No wonder most of the trading today is done with money! (See MONEY; TRADE.)

Spearheads

Fur

Beads

BASEBALL The game of baseball is considered the national sport of the United States. On one day every season even the president of the United States takes part in a game. He throws a baseball out on the diamond to begin the first big-league game of the season in Washington, D. C.

Almost every American understands baseball because almost everyone has played the game himself. Most schools have baseball teams, and baseball games are common on playgrounds or empty lots on summer afternoons.

In Cooperstown, N. Y., there is a baseball Hall of Fame. It was built at Cooperstown because Abner Doubleday laid out the first real diamond there in 1839. But games much like baseball were played long before 1839. Probably no one person should be called the inventor of baseball. It simply grew out of earlier games.

The game, of course, is a team game. There are nine players on each team. An ordinary game has nine innings. But if there is a tie at the end of the ninth inning, extra innings are played. In each inning each team has a turn at bat until three players have been put out.

Baseballs and bats are very carefully made. The balls are made of cork, rubber, yarn, and horsehide. They weigh about 5 ounces and are about 9 inches around. Baseball bats are usually made of ash wood. They cannot be longer than 42 inches, or thicker than 2-3/4 inches.

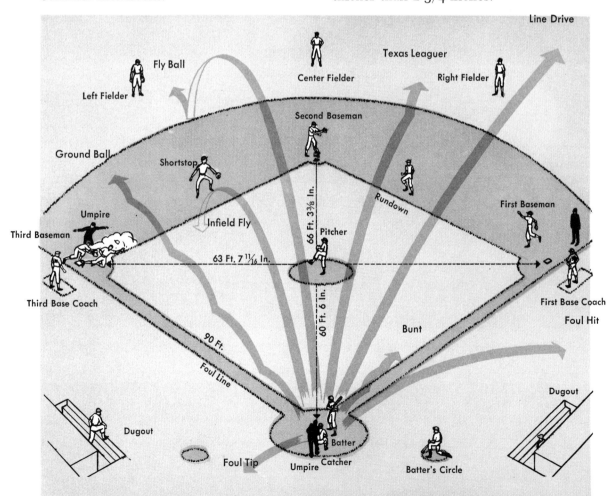

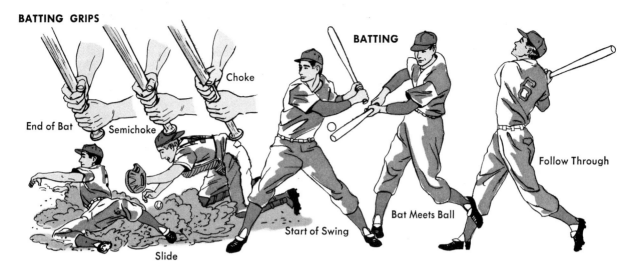

BATTING GRIPS

Choke

End of Bat Semichoke

BATTING

Follow Through

Start of Swing

Bat Meets Ball

Slide

In the United States there are many baseball leagues. The two major leagues are the National League and the American League. At the end of the season the winners in these two leagues play the World Series. There are many minor leagues. The players on all the teams in the major and minor leagues are paid for playing.

There are now leagues for young boys. The Little League, founded in 1939 in Williamsport, Pa., is for boys from 9 to 12.

This league even has its own World Series. The distance between the bases in Little League baseball is only 60 feet. Bats and balls are smaller in Little League baseball, too. But the game is played just like regular baseball.

Softball is a kind of baseball. It is played with a ball that is bigger and softer than a standard baseball. The bases are closer together. But the rules are very much like regular baseball rules.

PITCHING

Windup

Delivery

Follow Through

Fielding Fly Ball

Open Fielding Stance

PITCHING GRIPS

Knuckle Ball

Fast or curve balls are thrown with the grip shown in A and B.

A

B

BASKETBALL Every year more Americans pay to watch basketball games than to watch any other sport. There are a great many basketball teams. Almost every high school has one. So does almost every college. Besides, there are teams that play for money. They are like the major-league baseball teams. These teams play professional basketball.

Basketball is a truly American game. It was invented in 1891 by Dr. James Naismith, a teacher in the Y.M.C.A. College in Springfield, Mass. He wanted an indoor ball game to fill in between the football and baseball seasons. He wanted, too, a game that would not be too strenuous for older men to play.

Dr. Naismith fastened peach baskets high on the walls of the gymnasium. These baskets gave the new game its name. Of course, the object of the game was to get the ball into the baskets, or "make a basket." At first the bottoms were left in the baskets. After a player made a basket, someone had to bring a ladder to get the ball out again.

Dr. Naismith made careful plans to keep the game from being rough. If a player were allowed to run with the ball, he would have to be stopped by being held or pushed. So the rules said that a player could not run with the ball. It had to be thrown. Neither could a player take a ball away from another in any rough way.

At first basketball was considered "sissy stuff." But soon it became a very fast game —not at all easy for older people to play.

Any number of players, then nine, and then eight were on each team. But the number was soon cut down to five. Rule changes were made, too. Now, for instance, the ball can be dribbled, or bounced, forward.

Basketball courts are not all the same size. Junior courts are smaller than senior courts. Basketball games are not all the same length, either. High school teams play four 8-minute periods with a 10-minute rest at half time. College and professional teams play two 20-minute halves separated by a 15-minute rest. In most professional games each half is divided into two 10-minute quarters.

In early games scores were rather low. But changes in the rules made higher scores possible. Now professional teams often score more than 100 points in a game.

Girls began playing basketball in the early 1900's. Today more than a million girls in the United States play it. The rules for girls are not just the same as the rules for boys and men. But many girls' teams choose to play by the boys' rules.

Basketball spread rapidly to other lands. Now it is played almost everywhere. Basketball teams from many parts of the world play in the Olympic games.

In many countries basketball has become an outdoor game. But in the United States it is still played mostly indoors.

BASKETS The idea of weaving such things as twigs and straw together to make baskets is a very old idea. Pieces of a basket made 6,000 years ago were found buried in the sand in Egypt. Probably baskets were made long before that.

When we think of baskets, we think of something to carry a small load in. But for centuries baskets have served other purposes, too.

Baskets have been used as cooking vessels. A basket can be woven so tightly that it will hold water. Food can be cooked in it if hot stones are dropped into the water.

In the Bible story the baby Moses was put in a basket for the princess of Egypt to find. Baskets have been used for cradles.

Baskets have served as hats. They have been used to catch fish. They have been used to store grain and to sift corn meal. Big baskets have even been used as boats.

Baskets serve many purposes.

Bamboo stalks, willow twigs, tree roots, strips of bark, and palm leaves are some of the materials used in basketmaking. Reeds, grass, and straw are others.

The easiest way of making a basket is simply to weave strips of thin wood or bark into a mat, and then bend the mat up into shape. Many ordinary market baskets are now made by machine in that way. Better baskets can be made by either twining or coiling. A twined basket has a framework shaped much like the framework of an umbrella. Grass or something similar is woven around the framework. In a coiled basket the framework material itself is coiled round and round. The coils are held together with some grasslike material.

CALIFORNIA INDIAN BASKETS

In the beginning, basketmakers were trying only to make something useful. But in time some of them wanted to make their baskets beautiful, too.

Many tribes of American Indians grew to be clever basketmakers. They decorated some of their baskets with shells or beads or feathers. They wove designs in colored straw into many of them, too. Different designs have such names as arrowhead, butterfly, and striped water snake.

Among the most beautiful baskets ever made are the feather-covered sun baskets of the Pomo Indians of California. There are not many sun baskets. The Indians burned most of them to honor their dead.

BATS Many people are afraid of all bats. But they should not be. The only bats known to harm people are the vampire bats of South America. These bats live on blood. The wounds they make are small, but if a person or an animal is bitten a great many times he may become ill. The many other kinds of bats are not at all dangerous. Some even make good pets.

Most bats are tiny creatures. Our common little brown bat weighs only about as much as a nickel. But the bat called the flying fox, which lives in the tropics, has a wingspread of five feet.

Bats fly, but they are not birds. They are mammals instead. They have fur, and they feed their babies milk.

The wings of a bat are made of tough skin. The skin is stretched from the animal's "arms" and long fingers to its hind legs and tail.

Bats are swift and expert flyers. Even in the dark a bat can fly about without bumping into anything. It has a kind of sonar system. As it flies it makes sounds that are too high-pitched for us to hear. These sounds are echoed by anything in the way. The bat's big ears catch the echoes. The bat then flies in another direction.

Vampire bats are the only bats that live on blood. Some bats eat fruit, but most bats live chiefly on insects. The insect-eating bats are a big help to us because they eat mosquitoes and other insects that are harmful. These bats catch some insects simply by flying with their mouths open. They catch others in folds of their wings. They reach back from time to time to eat the insects they have caught in their "nets." Bats drink water by scooping it up with their tongues as they fly over it.

As a rule, bats sleep during the daytime and fly about after the sun sets. To sleep they hang themselves upside down in a hollow tree, a cave, or a crack in a building.

There are many foolish beliefs about bats. "As blind as a bat" is a common saying, but bats have good eyesight. Another wrong idea is that bats carry bedbugs. Still another is that a bat will fly straight at the head of any woman that comes near. No one knows how such ideas got started.

Silver-haired Bat

Big-eared Bat

Little Brown Bat

BAY A bay is an arm of a lake or a sea. It is like a gulf except that a gulf is usually larger. Hudson Bay, on the northern coast of North America, is much larger than most bays. Massachusetts Bay, Delaware Bay, Chesapeake Bay, and San Francisco Bay are four of the bays along the shores of the United States.

BEAR Almost everyone knows a bear when he sees one. One of the first stories children hear is the story of Goldilocks and the three bears. And toy bears can be bought in almost any toy store.

There are many common sayings about bears. "Clumsy as a bear," "shaggy as a bear," "hungry as a bear," "cross as a bear," and "bear hug" are a few of them. Not all these sayings are fair to these big animals.

Bears look clumsy, especially when they walk on their hind legs. But they are not nearly as clumsy as they look. They can run as fast as a pony. Some kinds of bears can climb a tree as fast as a squirrel.

Bears certainly are shaggy. They have very heavy coats of fur. In winter their heavy coats are a wonderful protection from the cold.

Bears do have big appetites. In zoos they try all sorts of tricks to make the visitors give them something to eat. In Yellowstone Park the bears appear to be always looking for food. They visit people's camps and take any food they can find. They seem to like honey and bacon especially well, but they will eat almost anything people eat. The rangers in the park say that the bears are fed "combination salad." "Combination salad" is the rangers' name for the scraps from the hotel kitchens.

Bear cubs are playful; they are seldom "cross as a bear." Some grown bears are playful, too. But no grown bear can really be counted on to be friendly. And their strong "arms" and sharp claws are dangerous weapons. Bears do not kill anything by hugging. There is no true "bear hug."

Many bears sleep during cold weather. Baby bears are born then. There are usually two of them. Baby bears are tiny and very helpless. The mother bear takes good care of them.

Until about 100 years ago trained bears were common in many parts of the world. Wandering showmen often had trained bears, just as the organ-grinders of more recent times often had trained monkeys. Bears can be trained to do many clever tricks partly because they can walk about on their hind legs.

Bears, as their fur shows, are mammals. They are found in many parts of the world. The spectacled bear of South America, the sun bear of Malaya, and the honey bear of India are a few of the different kinds.

The pictures show two of the bears found in America. Black bears live in forests in many parts of North America. Cinnamon bears are merely "blond" black bears. Grizzly bears, noted for their

Black Bear

Black Bear Cubs

Grizzly Bear

strength and fierceness, live in the western mountains.

The Far North is the home of the polar bears. A polar bear may live its whole life on a cake of ice and in the cold water around the ice.

The biggest bears are the Alaskan brown bears. They are the biggest land animals that eat meat. An Alaskan brown bear may weigh three-quarters of a ton. But none of the bears living today are as large as the giant cave bears that lived during the great Ice Age.

The Ice Age bears died out, and many people fear that the bears of today will someday disappear. Even now there are few grizzly bears left. The Florida black bear has become rare, too.

In the sky there are two constellations called the Great Bear and the Little Bear. The people of long ago thought that the stars in these constellations made pictures of bears. The tails of these animals in the sky show especially well. It is queer that people called them bears, for real bears have stub tails.

They have four long, sharp teeth that are like chisels. To cut down a tree a beaver gnaws around and around it. The beaver works until it has cut a deep ring around the tree. When the tree shivers, the beaver slaps the ground with its tail. The slap warns other beavers that the tree is about to fall. Down it comes! Now many beavers work together cutting it into pieces.

Beavers cut down trees not only to build dams and homes, but also to get food. They eat the bark of the trees. They may also eat the wood itself. The beavers store logs and branches in the water near their homes. They pile stones on the branches to hold them down. Poplar trees make the best food for beavers.

BEAVER Men were not the first builders of dams. Beavers built dams long before men did. Beavers are clever engineers.

Beavers build their homes in ponds. The dams they build hold back the water in streams and make it form ponds. There may be 25 or 30 beaver homes in one pond formed by a beaver dam.

These animal engineers work together to build their dams. They pile up logs and twigs, weight them down with stones, and fasten them in place with mud. They pat the mud into the cracks with their noses and feet. They work on a dam until it is so solid and high that very little water goes through it or over it.

Beavers build their homes, too, of branches, twigs, and mud. One of these homes looks like a big pile of branches out in a pond. It is really a one-room house with doors in the floor. Beavers must swim down into the water to get in or out.

To get logs for their homes and dams, beavers cut down trees. They belong to the group of gnawing mammals, or rodents.

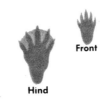

Front

Hind

Beaver dams create ponds in which the beavers build their houses.

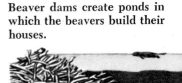

Some of the beavers in a pond may live by themselves in homes in the bank instead of in "log" houses. The homes in the bank are long tunnels.

During the winter beavers stay in their homes most of the time. They leave their homes only to get food from their storehouses. But when spring comes they are "as busy as beavers" again.

Beavers have beautiful fur. To get their fur we have killed far too many beavers for our own good. For beavers, while they are building dams to help themselves, are helping us, too. Their dams hold back water, prevent floods, and keep good farmland from being washed away. The soil that they save for us is worth much more than their fur. (See CONSERVATION; RODENTS.)

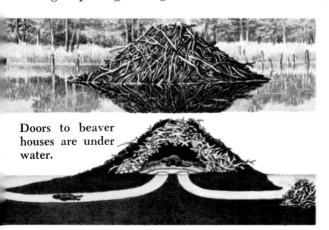

Doors to beaver houses are under water.

BEE People have eaten honey for thousands of years. They had honey long before they had sugar. Honey is made by honeybees. The bees make it from nectar, the sweet juice found in flowers.

The first honey people ate came from wild bees. Finding a bee tree—a hollow tree where wild bees had stored honey for themselves—used to be an important happening. There are still many wild bees. But now most of our honey comes from bees that live in man-made hives built especially for them.

Honeybees live in big groups. There may be more than 75,000 in one hive. A hive of bees is somewhat like a city. Some bees do one kind of work. Other bees do other kinds. They work together and help one another.

In every hive there is a queen bee that lays eggs. Some of the bees in a hive are drones. Drones are male bees. Most of the bees in a hive are workers. The workers are female bees, but they do not lay eggs. They do not have "children."

The job of many of the worker bees is to gather nectar for honey. The bees that gather nectar also gather pollen from the flowers. Pollen, too, makes good bee food.

Bumblebee

Sweat Bee

Red Clover

There are many other kinds of bees. But none of the others is so important to us as the honeybees and bumblebees.

Some workers build honeycomb out of wax that comes from their bodies. Some workers take care of the queen. Some feed the baby bees. Some fan air into the hive. Others keep the hive clean. Still others guard the hive. They sting any enemy that comes near.

A honeybee, like many other insects, goes through great changes as it grows up. First it is an egg. The egg hatches into a wormlike larva. The larva becomes a pupa. The pupa changes to a full-grown bee.

A few of the baby bees in a hive are fed nothing but a special food called royal jelly. These baby bees are to be queens. When a young queen bee grows up, the old queen leaves the hive. Many of the workers go with her to a new home.

Honeybees help us by making honey. They help in another way, too. As they go about gathering nectar and pollen, they carry pollen from flower to flower. By carrying pollen they help seeds form.

Bumblebees, too, make honey, but we do not eat their honey. They are a big help, however, because they carry pollen.

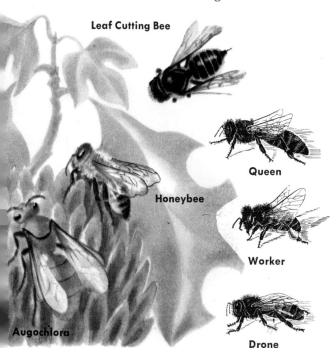

Leaf Cutting Bee

Queen

Honeybee

Worker

Augochlora

Drone

BEETHOVEN, (BAY tow ven) **LUDWIG VAN** (1770-1827) About 130 years ago a musician sat quietly at a concert in Vienna while his new symphony was played for the first time. At the end he had to face the audience to know that they were clapping wildly. He was totally deaf. The musician was Beethoven, one of the greatest composers who ever lived.

Beethoven wrote about 300 pieces of music. Some of his most beautiful pieces he wrote after he became deaf.

It is hard for anyone to be deaf. But probably it is worse for a composer than for anyone else. Think of not being able to hear the music you have written!

Even as a child Beethoven did not have a happy life. His father, who was a singer with the court band in Bonn, Germany, drank a great deal, and was lazy besides. When the boy was only four, his father decided to make a musician of him. Hour after hour Beethoven had to practice on the violin and the clavier. Whenever he did not work hard, his father was cruel.

It is a wonder that the boy did not hate music. But he did not. He learned so fast that he was able to make a concert tour when he was only 11. When he was 17, the great Mozart praised him.

A few years later Beethoven went to Vienna to study with Haydn. Soon he was writing a great deal of music himself.

Beethoven had an ugly face and a very bad temper. But he also had a great deal of charm. The wealthy people of Vienna invited him time after time to their homes. They forgave him when his temper flared up. Illness made him become deaf when he was only 31. During the rest of his life he was often ill. He was often worried about money, too.

Beethoven wrote long compositions and short ones, gay ones and sad ones, gentle ones and exciting ones. His nine symphonies are among his masterpieces. (See COMPOSERS; MUSIC; ORCHESTRA.)

BEETLES All the insects pictured on these pages are beetles. The whole book could be filled with pictures of beetles, for there are many, many kinds. If you were to study a different kind of beetle every day in the year, it would take you 60 years to study them all.

As a rule, a beetle has two pairs of wings. The front wings are hard. They make a smooth cover for the insect's body. The back wings are thin. Most beetles keep their thin wings folded up under their hard wings unless they are flying.

Beetles go through several stages during their lives. They are first eggs, then larvas, then pupas, and then adults. Some larvas are often called grubs.

Many beetles are good friends of ours. Others are insect pests.

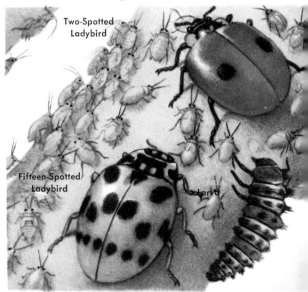

Two-Spotted Ladybird

Fifteen-Spotted Ladybird

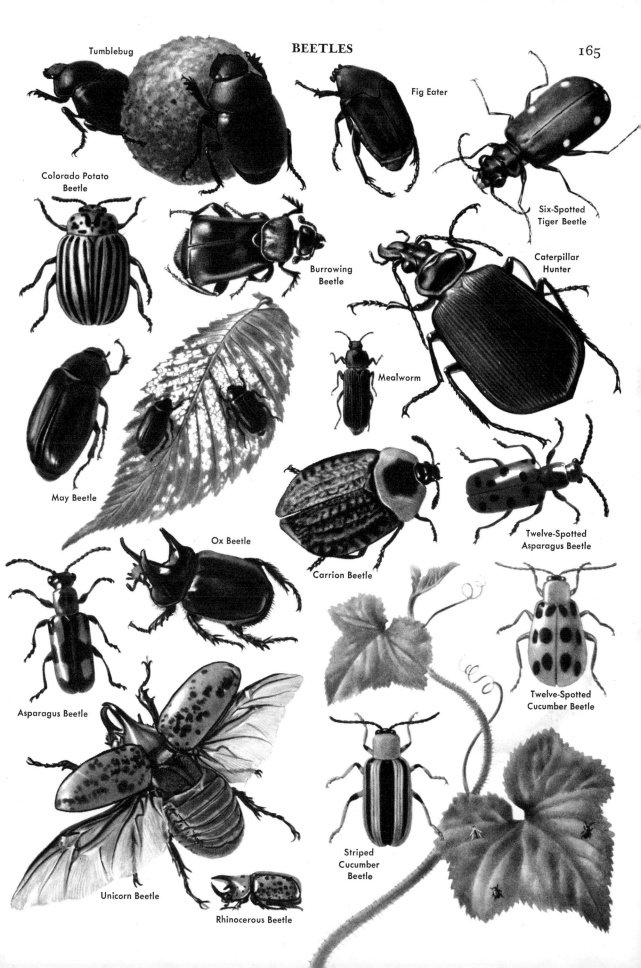

Tumblebug

Fig Eater

Colorado Potato Beetle

Six-Spotted Tiger Beetle

Burrowing Beetle

Caterpillar Hunter

Mealworm

May Beetle

Twelve-Spotted Asparagus Beetle

Ox Beetle

Carrion Beetle

Asparagus Beetle

Twelve-Spotted Cucumber Beetle

Unicorn Beetle

Striped Cucumber Beetle

Rhinocerous Beetle

BELGIUM

NORTH SEA

NETHERLANDS

Ostend • Bruges
Merksem
Turnhout o
Deurne
Hoboken o
ANTWERP
Saint-Nicolas o
• Ghent
Alost o
Mechlin o
Genk o
Roulers o
Courtrai o
Anderlecht ● BRUSSELS
Louvain o
Hasselt o
Mouscron o
Forest Uccle
B E L G I U M
Liége o
Seraing o Verviers o
Namur o
Meuse River
GERMANY

Ourthe River

Belgian Flag

FRANCE

ELEVATION
Feet
2000-5000
1000-2000
0-1000

MILES
0   50

Coat of Arms

Coal
Machinery
Household Appliances
Smelting
Textiles
Shipping
Chemicals
Dairying
Garden Crops

Total population................8,951,443
Area (square miles)............11,779

BELGIUM Few countries of the whole world are more crowded than small Belgium. It is almost as crowded as its next-door neighbor—the Netherlands.

The northwestern part of Belgium is called Flanders. It is a lowland bordering the North Sea. The southeastern part of Belgium is hilly and high. The Belgians of Flanders speak Flemish, a language much like Dutch. The Belgians of the highlands speak French.

A hundred years before Columbus discovered America many cities in Flanders were famous for weaving woolen and linen cloth and other textiles. Ghent was the chief city for woolens. In those days it was a much bigger city than London. Bruges (BROOZH) was the main port. Through it the textiles made in Flanders traveled to other lands.

Bruges was not on the coast. It was safer from pirates than if it had been. Ships had

to come up a small river to it. But in time this river was choked with mud. Ships began going to Antwerp instead of to Bruges. In the 1500's, Antwerp was the greatest port in Flanders. In fact, it was the greatest trading center in the world.

But Antwerp soon had its troubles. It stands on the Schelde (SKEL de) River. The mouth of this river is not in Belgium, but in the Netherlands. Beginning in 1713, the Dutch refused to let boats travel up the river to Flanders. Then Antwerp lost much of its trade. Long wars, too, did great harm to the region. Many workers from the textile towns went to other countries. The once-thriving cities of Flanders became almost dead cities.

But many of these cities came to life again in the 1800's. Today Antwerp is one of the busiest ports in Europe. Ships can reach it easily. Many railroads lead to it and to other Belgian ports. About 25,000 ships dock in Belgium each year. And once again Flemish cities are famous for their fine textiles.

Not all the people of Flanders are textile workers. About half of them are farmers. Most of their farms are small, much like big gardens. But a farmer makes his two or three acres produce a great deal. Many of the crops are root crops such as sugar beets and potatoes. Some farmers raise flax, used in making linen.

On the highlands most of the people are farmers. But the land is not very fertile, and much of it is in pasture.

The most crowded part of all Belgium is where the highlands and the lowland meet. This part of Belgium is often called "the Trough." Here there is a coal field with great iron and steel mills. There are thousands of other factories, too. Cities are so close together that it is hard to tell where one ends and the next begins. The biggest of these cities is Liège (le EZH).

Brussels, the capital, is Belgium's largest city. It is almost in the center of the country. All the signs there are in both French and Flemish. Some of the buildings of Brussels are centuries old and very beautiful. They help remind people of the early glory of Flanders.

For hundreds of years, Belgium was ruled by other countries—Spain, the Netherlands, and France. In 1831 the country won its independence from the Netherlands and chose its first king—Leopold I. It has had a king ever since.

In Africa Belgium has a colony 80 times as big as Belgium itself. This colony is the Belgian Congo. It lies along the great Congo River. Much of the Belgian Congo is covered with thick forest. It has great stores of minerals—gold, diamonds, tin, uranium, and, above all, copper. The minerals of this colony will help keep Belgium an important country. (See FLAX; IRON AND STEEL; LACE; LINEN; TEXTILES; SPINNING AND WEAVING; WOOL; WORLD WAR I; WORLD WAR II.)

Gothic Guild Houses—Antwerp

Lacemaking

Fried Potato Wagon

The Cloth Hall Ypres

Old Harbor Ostend

Delivering Milk

Canal Scene Bruges

BELL, ALEXANDER GRAHAM (1847-1922)

In 1876, at a world's fair in Philadelphia, a young inventor had a new invention on display. For a time no one paid much attention to it. But one day Dom Pedro, the emperor of Brazil, saw the invention. He thought it was wonderful. The invention was the telephone. The inventor was a young man named Alexander Graham Bell.

Bell was born in Scotland. His father was a teacher of deaf-mutes. When Alexander grew up, he taught deaf-mutes, too.

In 1870 Bell moved to Canada and soon afterward to Boston. In Boston he taught deaf-and-dumb children during the day. At night he worked on his hobby—electricity.

Bell had an idea for a new kind of telegraph instrument. It would send six messages at once. He called it the "harmonic" telegraph. He took his plan to an electrical shop in Boston. Thomas Watson, a workman in the shop, was given the job of building the instrument. When it was finished, Bell was not pleased. He went to the shop to say that his directions had not been followed. There he met Watson for the first time. The meeting was the beginning of a friendship that lasted for years.

For many long nights after this Bell and Watson worked together on the telegraph. Bell was sure his idea was good. But he could not get the telegraph to work well.

Bell and Watson had long talks. One of the things they talked about was a possible way of sending speech over electric wires.

About six months after Bell and Watson began working together, Bell heard a peculiar sound on his telegraph set. Watson was working at the other end of the line. Bell rushed into the room where Watson was working and asked him what he had done. Watson showed him how he had plucked the spring of his set. Bell saw at once how the sound he had heard had been made. Now he knew at last how a telephone could be built! The very next day he and Watson had the first telephone ready to try.

The telephone was not a success at the start. Much more work had to be done on it. But the following spring, on March 10, 1876, Bell said these now famous words into the telephone: "Mr. Watson, come here; I want you." Watson heard it—the first sentence ever heard over the telephone.

Thirty-nine years later the first telephone line between New York and San Francisco was opened. Bell in New York talked to Watson in San Francisco. He used a model of his first telephone. He said again, "Mr. Watson, come here; I want you."

Bell worked on many other inventions. But he will always be remembered as the inventor of the telephone. His patent on the telephone has been called the most valuable patent ever issued. (See TELEPHONE.)

BELLS In a lonely mountain pasture a bell tinkles. It tells the shepherd where his sheep are. A big dinner bell calls the farmer in from the field to dinner. In a tower a tune is played with many bells. Telephones keep ringing in a busy office. Church bells, doorbells, sleigh bells, fire alarms, bell buoys, alarm clocks: bells mean a great deal to us.

The idea of bells is old. More than 2,000 years ago Jewish priests wore little bells on their robes. The kings of ancient Persia wore bells for decoration, too. The Chinese also had bells long ago. But big bells were not much used until about 1,500 years ago. Builders then began to put bell towers on churches so that the bells could call people to worship.

From then on bells were used more and more. Town criers rang bells when they had news to tell. Curfew bells told boys and girls when they must be in for the night. Clocks struck the hours on bells. Many cities built bell towers.

Bells are made of many kinds of material. Glass, china, wood, and metal are among them. Most big bells are made of bronze. Some beautiful small bells are made of silver.

A bell makes its sound when it is struck. Many bells are struck by clappers which hang down inside them. These bells ring when they are swung. Some bells have balls inside. These bells ring when they are shaken. Other bells are rung without being moved. They are struck by hammers.

It is not easy to make a bell with a beautiful, clear tone. To make a bell of bronze, the bellmaker first makes a mold of clay. Then he pours melted bronze into the mold. The metal hardens. Making a bell in this way is called casting a bell. After a bell comes out of its mold, the bellmaker tries it. If he is not pleased with its tone, he may shave off a little metal here and there. He may even melt the bronze and start all over again.

Every bell has its own note. But long ago the people of Europe found that they could play tunes if they had several bells that gave off different notes. People learned to ring bells just as they learned to play the violin. Each bell, as a rule, had a rope hanging from it. The player pulled one rope after another.

Now bells are sometimes put together in groups called carillons. A carillon is not played by pulling ropes. Instead, the player pushes down keys somewhat like the keys of an organ. One of the famous carillons in the United States is in the Singing Tower in Florida.

The biggest bell ever made was never rung. A piece broke out of it before it could be. This bell is now standing in Moscow. People can go inside it. The bell is almost as tall as a two-story house. The biggest bell in use is in Moscow, too. Another very large bell is in a pagoda in Burma. The United States has a famous bell—the Liberty Bell. (See LIBERTY BELL.)

BERLIN The city of Berlin is the largest city in Germany. As great cities of the Old World go, it is young. There has been a Berlin for centuries, but it grew into a really big city less than 100 years ago. Now it is one of the ten largest cities in the world.

It is not hard to understand why Berlin was long in becoming a great city. The northern part of Germany is a lowland that reaches the North Sea and the Baltic. The southern part is mostly highland. Many German cities grew up along the coast. They sent out fishing fleets. Ships brought goods from other lands. Other German cities grew up where the highlands and the lowland joined. There the soil is rich. There, too, products of the highlands were traded for goods from the lowland and the northern ports. But Berlin is in the middle of the lowland. The land round about was not good farmland. Much of it was swampy.

But in time a great deal of the lowland around Berlin was drained. Much of the drained land was made into good farmland.

Before 1871 there were many small separate states in Germany. In that year they were joined to form one strong nation. Berlin was made the capital. Of course, being made the capital helped it to grow.

A canal dug between the Elbe and the Oder rivers helped Berlin to grow, too. By way of the canal boats could reach the city from both the North Sea and the Baltic.

Perhaps more important still, Germany began to change from a farming country to a manufacturing country. Berlin was in a good location for manufacturing.

When Berlin began to grow, it grew like a mushroom. Railroads spread out in all directions. Factories sprang up for making such things as tools and chemicals and clothing. Government buildings, hotels, theaters, a university, an opera house, and beautiful stores and homes were built.

Berlin was heavily bombed in World War II. Many, perhaps half, of its buildings were destroyed. At the end of the war it was divided into four zones. France, Britain, the United States, and the Soviet Union were each given control of one zone. The zone controlled by the Soviet Union is called East Berlin. The rest is West Berlin. The Brandenburg Gate separates the two. In East Berlin, Unter den Linden, a world-famous street named for its linden trees, still lies in ruins. The Tiergarten, once the royal hunting grounds, is in West Berlin. It, too, was ruined by the war, but is now a beautiful public park.

There are many problems for a city divided as Berlin is. It is hard to guess what its future will be. (See CITIES; GERMANY.)

Though divided, Berlin has remained an important city.

Bicycles are popular for traveling around Bermuda.

BERMUDAS About 600 miles east of the coast of North Carolina there is a group of more than 350 tiny islands. People live on only 20 of them. These islands are the Bermudas. Juan de Bermúdez, a Spanish explorer, discovered them in 1519.

Sometimes the Bermudas are called the paradise of the Atlantic. The scenery is beautiful, and the climate is delightful.

The chief business of the islands is taking care of tourists. There are many good hotels and beautiful beaches. Visitors can go boating and fishing to their heart's content. There are big-game fish to be caught in the waters round about.

The soil is thin. In fact, to make a "paved" road, all that needs to be done is to scrape off a thin layer of soil. Under it there is a layer of white limestone. Most of the buildings are built of this white limestone. Even the roofs are made of it. Many of the roofs are built to catch and hold rain water, for fresh water is scarce in the Bermudas. There are very few wells.

Only about a third of the 40,000 people there are white. The rest are Negroes.

The people of the islands raise one unusual crop—Easter lilies. Many of these lilies are shipped to the United States.

The islands belong to Britain. But Britain has let the United States set up big air and naval bases there.

BERRIES Seed plants wrap up their seeds in many different kinds of seed packages. One kind of seed package is called a berry. In all berries the seeds are surrounded by pulp and a soft skin.

The picture shows five kinds of berries. It may be a surprise to find that grapes and tomatoes are berries. But a careful look tells that they are very much like gooseberries, cranberries, and blueberries.

Many berries are good to eat. But not all berries are. Some of those that are not good to eat are very pretty to look at.

Names do not always tell a true story. We call some fruits berries that really are not. Strawberries are not true berries. Their seeds are on the outside. Raspberries and blackberries are not true berries, either. Each tiny seed has its own wrapping of pulp and skin. (See FRUITS; GRAPES.)

Grapes

Gooseberries

Cranberries

Blueberries

Tomatoes

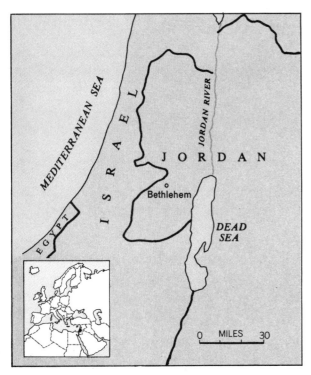

BETHLEHEM "Oh, Little Town of Bethlehem" has long been one of the best-loved Christmas carols. It tells of the birth of Jesus in Bethlehem.

The town, which now has about 19,000 people in it, lies on a hill covered with vineyards and olive groves. It is not far from the city of Jerusalem.

Bethlehem has one long street. It leads to the Church of the Nativity, which stands at the spot where Jesus is believed to have been born. Many beautiful gifts have been given to this famous church.

Thousands of people visit Bethlehem every year. Many Christians think of it as the most sacred spot in the whole world. (See CHRISTIANITY; CHRISTMAS; HOLY LAND; JERUSALEM; JESUS.)

BIBLE Almost every religion has its sacred writings. The sacred writings of the Christian religion make up the Bible.

The Bible is many books in one. The many books are divided into the Old Testament and the New Testament. Each book is broken up into chapters, and each chapter into verses.

The Old Testament is sacred to Jews as well as to Christians. It tells the story of the Hebrew people. In it, too, are the teachings of the Hebrew prophets.

The first book in the Old Testament is Genesis. "Genesis" means "the beginning." The names of many other Old Testament books are the names of prophets.

One of the most loved chapters in the Old Testament is the Twenty-third Psalm. It begins, "The Lord is my shepherd."

The New Testament tells the story of Jesus and his disciples. It tells, too, about the beginnings of the Christian church.

Most of the Old Testament was first written in Hebrew. A little of it was in Aramaic (ar a MAY ek). The New Testament was first written in Greek. About 1,500 years ago the whole Bible was translated into Latin. It has now been translated into hundreds of languages.

Different people who are trying to change a Hebrew or Greek or Latin sentence into English may use different words. It is easy to see, then, why there are different versions of the Bible. Different people have translated it into English.

The whole Bible was first translated into English in 1382. There have been many later translations. Millions and millions of English Bibles have been sold.

Even if the Bible were not sacred, many people would read it. Nowhere are there any better stories, or more beautiful poems, or letters, or prayers. Nowhere are there any wiser proverbs. The Bible is not only sacred. It is also great literature.

The shepherd boy David became king of the Jews.

BIBLE STORIES The Bible tells many stories. These are a few of them:

JOSEPH AND HIS BROTHERS

Joseph was the son of Jacob. Joseph's ten older brothers were jealous of him because he was their father's favorite. Jacob loved Joseph so much that he gave him a beautiful coat of many colors.

The brothers wished to get rid of Joseph. One day they seized him and sold him to some travelers on their way to Egypt.

In Egypt Joseph, when he grew up, won the favor of Pharoah (FARE oh), the ruler of the land. Pharoah put Joseph next to

him in power. In time there was a famine in the land where Joseph's father and brothers lived. The brothers came to Egypt to buy food. They did not know that Joseph was a great man in Egypt. They did not know that it was from him they would have to buy the food.

They did not even recognize Joseph when they were brought before him. But Joseph recognized his brothers. He could have punished them. Instead, he returned good for the evil they had done him. He sent them home to bring Jacob and their wives and children back with them. For many years afterward the family of Jacob lived happily in Egypt.

MOSES

Joseph and his family were Hebrews. After Joseph's time there came to be many Hebrews in Egypt. Pharaoh began to fear they would fight against the Egyptians and take over the country. To guard against losing his throne, Pharaoh ordered all the boy babies of the Hebrews to be killed.

The mother of one baby boy put the baby in a basket and hid the basket in the bulrushes that grew along the Nile near Phar-

These children all play important parts in Bible stories.

Samuel

Moses

Miriam

Joseph

Rebekah

Pharaoh's daughter found the baby Moses in the bulrushes.

aoh's palace. The baby's older sister Miriam stood near by to watch. A princess, the daughter of Pharaoh, found the baby. She took pity on him and lifted the basket from the water. Miriam then stepped forward and offered to bring a nurse to take care of the baby. She was told to do so. The nurse she brought was her mother.

The princess named the baby Moses. She raised him as her own son. He grew up to become a great leader of his people. It was Moses to whom God gave the Ten Commandments.

DANIEL IN THE LIONS' DEN

In the days when Nebuchadnezzar was king of Babylon, Daniel and many other Jewish children were taken to Babylon as captives. Some years later Darius, the king of Persia, conquered Babylon. Daniel was well liked by Darius. He was given a position of great importance.

But some of the other men of the court were jealous of Daniel and plotted against him. Through a trick they caused Darius to order that Daniel be thrown into a den of lions. The next morning, Darius hurried to the den of lions and called out to Daniel.

Daniel answered, "My God has sent His angel and has shut the lions' mouths, so that they have not hurt me." When Darius saw that Daniel was not harmed, he was very glad, and he ordered all of his people to worship Daniel's God.

DAVID AND GOLIATH

David was a shepherd boy. He became armor-bearer to Saul, the king of Israel. David and Jonathan, Saul's son, were friends. They were such good friends that either of them would gladly have died for the other.

Once, when Saul was at war with a neighboring kingdom, a giant came out from the camp of the enemy. His name was Goliath. Goliath dared anyone from Saul's camp to come out and fight him. All Saul's soldiers were afraid. But young David was not. He went out to meet the giant, armed with only a slingshot and five round stones from a brook. But he shot a stone right between the eyes of Goliath and killed him. When Saul died, David became king of Israel.

WALLS OF JERICHO

These four stories come from the Old Testament. The New Testament tells about Jesus and his disciples. It tells, too, the story of Paul, the first great missionary of the Christian church. (See BABYLONIA; EGYPT; ISRAEL; JESUS; JEWS; NOAH'S ARK; PERSIA; TEN COMMANDMENTS; TWELVE DISCIPLES.)

Armed with only a stone, the young David killed the mighty Goliath.

The first bicycle was a walking bicycle.

BICYCLES AND MOTORCYCLES Bicycles are well named. Their name means "two wheels."

No one knows who first had the idea of a bicycle. One of the earliest bicycles we know about was made by Baron Karl Drais, a German. He called it a draisine.

The draisine was introduced into England in 1818. This bicycle had no pedals. It was made of two wheels joined by a wooden bar. The rider sat on the bar and kicked the ground to push himself along. The draisine was nicknamed the "dandy horse" because young English dandies liked to ride this new contraption.

Twenty-five years or so later a Scotchman, Kirkpatrick MacMillan, built the first bicycle with pedals. The pedals turned the back wheel. No one paid much attention to this bicycle, although its inventor was arrested for "furious driving."

In 1866 a Frenchman, Pierre Lallement, was given the first patent for a bicycle. His bicycle was nicknamed a "boneshaker" because it jolted the rider so much. Its pedals were attached to the front wheel.

This is an early version of a motorcycle.

Someone then got the idea that a bicycle would go faster if the front wheel were bigger. Bicycles were made with front wheels almost as tall as a man and with very small back wheels. These bicycles did go fast, but they were hard to mount and to balance.

Then came bicycles with a big back wheel and a small front wheel. They were not easy to ride, either.

Finally bicycle makers went back to the idea of having two wheels of the same size. But the new bicycles were very much better than the early bicycles built on that plan. The rider, by pushing pedals, made a chain turn the back wheel. The chain was arranged so that turning the pedals once made the back wheel turn more than once around. These "safety" bicycles could go as fast as the big-wheeled ones. Improvements then came rapidly. Air-filled rubber tires, coaster brakes, and speed gears were a few of them. When safety bicycles were new, bicycles for two were a fad. There were even some bicycles for four riders.

Today many boys and girls in the United States have "bikes." Not many grown people do. In Europe the story is different. There, many grown people ride bicycles to work. It is a common sight in some cities to see the streets crowded with bicycles at the end of a working day.

Motorcycles are bicycles that are driven by engines. The engines are much like automobile engines except that they are smaller. Motor scooters are driven by very simple gasoline engines.

Motorcycles are cheaper to buy than automobiles and much cheaper to run. Sometimes they have a sidecar for an extra passenger. Many cities have motorcycle police. Motorcycles are useful for delivering small articles. They are also useful in war because they are speedy and use little gasoline.

There are motorcycle races, often up steep hills. In carnivals, motorcycle riders often do daredevil stunts. But for everyday fun motorcycles cannot take the place of common "bikes."

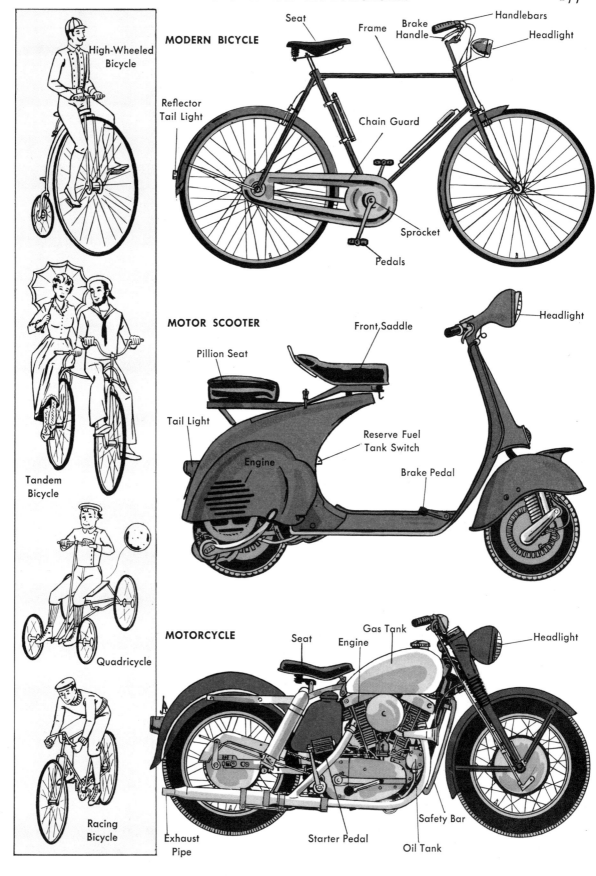

High-Wheeled Bicycle

Tandem Bicycle

Quadricycle

Racing Bicycle

MODERN BICYCLE

Seat
Frame
Brake Handle
Handlebars
Headlight
Reflector Tail Light
Chain Guard
Sprocket
Pedals

MOTOR SCOOTER

Front Saddle
Headlight
Pillion Seat
Tail Light
Reserve Fuel Tank Switch
Engine
Brake Pedal

MOTORCYCLE

Gas Tank
Seat
Engine
Headlight
Exhaust Pipe
Starter Pedal
Oil Tank
Safety Bar

Cave men hunted with rocks and spears.

BIG-GAME HUNTING The men in the picture below are all big-game hunters. But they are hunting in different ways. The hunters on the elephant have guns and are about to shoot a tiger. Another has just caught a leopard in a trap. He will take this big animal back alive to a zoo. Still another hunter has a movie camera. He is taking pictures of big animals in the places where they live naturally.

Big-game hunting is not new. Even cave men went big-game hunting. They had to. They needed food. Besides, they had to protect themselves from wild animals. Of course, they did not have guns. They used rocks, clubs, spears, or bows and arrows.

Much later, when there were kings and countries, noblemen went big-game hunting for sport. A nobleman's greatness was measured partly by the number of wild animals he killed. In many countries lands came to be set aside for royal hunting.

Big-game hunting is still a sport. Not many people nowadays need to kill big wild animals for food or to protect themselves.

In early times men had to go only a little way from their homes to hunt big game. But now they must go to out-of-the-way places. Often they organize expeditions, or safaris (sa FA reez) and travel long distances. Much of the fun of big-game hunting is the adventure of going to faraway places. An American president, Theodore Roosevelt, was a famous big-game hunter.

People have killed so many animals for sport that big game is becoming scarce, even in out-of-the-way places. In many lands there are laws to protect the animals

Filming Wild Life

Trapping Live Animals

that are left. Areas have been set aside where they can live without being in danger from hunters. The bison and the grizzly bear are two big American animals that would probably have disappeared if they had not been protected.

The lion, the tiger, and all the other "big cats" are prizes of big-game hunters. These animals are all dangerous. So are the elephant, the African buffalo, the rhinoceros, and the big bears. The animals considered the least dangerous of the big-game animals are the deer and the antelopes.

"Bringing them back alive" and taking pictures of wild animals are rather new ways of hunting. These two ways of hunting take the hunters to out-of-the-way places just as hunting to kill does. And it is often much harder to catch an animal without hurting it or to take a good picture of it than it is to kill it.

Big-game hunters have helped us learn a great deal about wild animals. Those who have taken pictures have probably helped most. Moving pictures of wild animals in their native homes tell us more about the animals than we could possibly learn by

Hunting almost made the American bison extinct.

watching them in zoos or by seeing them mounted in museums. Of course, if animals could wish, they would wish that all hunters had cameras instead of traps or guns. (See BEAR; BISON; CAVE MEN; ELEPHANT; LION; RHINOCEROS; TIGER.)

Tiger Hunting

BIG TREE Almost everyone knows where there is a very big tree. It may be a maple tree or an elm or an oak. But trees like the big one in the picture grow to be far larger than any maple or elm or oak. They are true giants. One name for them is "big trees." Another name for them is "giant sequoias" (see QUOY uhs.)

The biggest of the big trees are four or five times as tall as most of our shade trees. Their trunks may be as much as 30 feet across. There is enough wood in one of them for a whole village of houses.

Many of the big trees now standing were living when Columbus discovered America. Some were living when Christ was born. Some were alive even back in the days of the Pyramids.

Big trees are conifers. They bear their seeds in cones, just as pines, firs, and spruces do. Their closest relatives are the redwood trees.

Giant sequoias are found only in parts of California. Most of them are in national forests. The men of the Forest Service guard them from forest fires, harmful insects, and tree diseases. If the big trees were not protected, there might soon be none left. (See CONIFERS; NATIONAL PARKS.)

BIOLOGY The science of biology is the study of living things. Scientists who work in this field are called biologists. Biology is so big that it has been divided up into different sciences. Botany is one of them. It is the study of plants. Zoology is another. It is the study of animals. Even these sciences are so big that they have been divided up into many others. (See BOTANY; PHYSIOLOGY; ZOOLOGY.)

BIRD MIGRATION During the summer there are barn swallows in almost all parts of the United States and Canada. They build nests and raise their young there. But early in the fall the swallows leave their summer homes. They fly south for the winter. Some go as far south as Argentina. A barn swallow's winter home may be several thousand miles from its summer home. In the spring the swallows make the long journey back to the north.

Many other birds spend the summers in one part of the world and the winters in another. The traveling of birds between their summer homes and their winter homes is called bird migration.

The champion bird traveler is the arctic tern. This bird flies every fall from the far north to the far south. It returns every spring. Its fall and spring journeys together may be 22,000 miles—almost as long as a trip around the world at the equator.

Some birds make remarkable nonstop flights. The golden plover may fly over the Atlantic Ocean for more than 2,000 miles without stopping for food or rest. The tiny hummingbird crosses the Gulf of Mexico in a 500-mile nonstop flight.

Birds run into many dangers as they migrate. Storms, electric wires, lighted buildings, and hunters are some of them. But migration is a help to the birds that make the journey safely. It lets them live the year round in the kind of region they are best fitted for. And it is a big help in getting food.

We do not see as many birds migrating as you would expect. Many birds fly at night and rest during the daytime.

Birds get ready for their journeys by eating a great deal. They go over their wing feathers. Some birds, moreover, gather into big groups before they start.

As the maps show, in North America there are four great flyways along which birds travel. The barn swallow follows the Mississippi Flyway. So do many ducks.

No one knows how migration came about or why some birds migrate and others

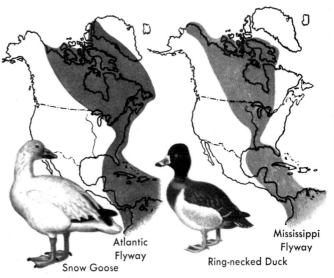

Atlantic Flyway
Snow Goose

Mississippi Flyway
Ring-necked Duck

do not. There are other mysteries about migration. No one knows how birds find their way. Probably landmarks such as rivers and mountains and coasts help. Air currents and the earth's magnetism may help, too. No one knows what starts birds on their spring and fall travels. Perhaps the amount of daylight they get each day lets them know when it is time to start.

Scientists are learning more and more about bird travels. Until a few years ago, for instance, the winter home of the chimney swift was unknown. In the fall the swifts flew out over the Gulf of Mexico, and no one saw them again until spring. Now it has been discovered that they spend the winters in Peru.

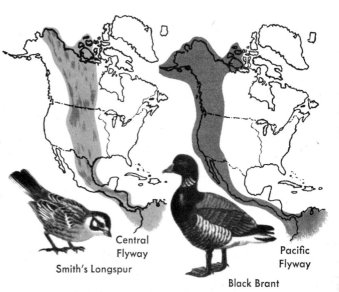

Central Flyway
Smith's Longspur

Pacific Flyway
Black Brant

Golden-
crowned
Kinglet

Yellow
Warbler

Redstart

Scarlet Tanager

Indigo
Bunting

Barn Swallow

Mallard Duck

BIRDS An ostrich is hundreds of times as big as a scarlet tanager. It weighs hundreds of times as much. An ostrich cannot fly. A scarlet tanager can fly for miles and miles without stopping to rest. An ostrich is dull-colored. A scarlet tanager is mostly bright red. But it is easy to see that an ostrich and a scarlet tanager are both birds. Their feathers tell that they are, for no other animals have feathers. All birds do have.

Ostrich

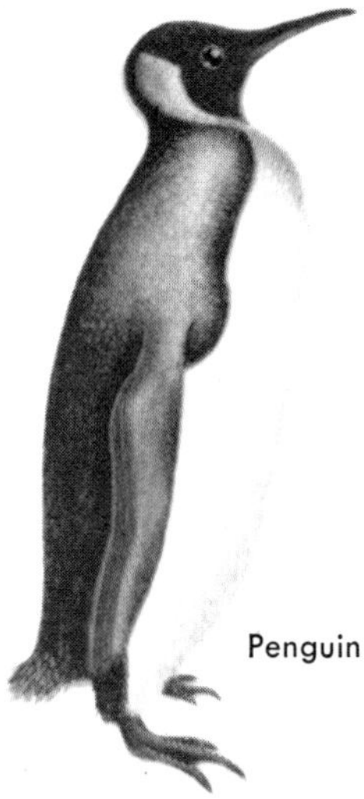

Penguin

Great Blue Heron

Cooper's Hawk

Cardinal

Rose-breasted
Grosbeak

Ruby-throated
Hummingbirds

Field Sparrow

Meadowlark

Birds are alike in other ways that are easy to see. They cannot all fly, but they all have two wings. They cannot all run about on the ground, but they all have two legs. They all, moreover, have bills.

Most birds are well fitted for flying. They are streamlined, and they are light in weight for their size. They are light partly because many of their bones are hollow. Besides, they have tiny air sacs scattered throughout their bodies. The air sacs act like little balloons. The feathers of the birds' wings and tail are a big help in flying. Their strong wing muscles are, too.

Like mammals, birds are warm blooded. Their bodies are even warmer than ours. Some birds have normal temperatures of as high as 112 degrees.

In the whole world there are about 14,-000 kinds of birds. There are about 800 in the United States.

A robin is much more like a bluebird than it is like a loon. In the same way, a hawk is much more like an eagle than it is like a woodpecker. Ways they are alike and ways they are different have been used to divide birds into groups. Among the many groups are the ducks, geese, and swans; the owls; and the parrots. Our songbirds are all in the very biggest bird group — the perching birds.

These baby cardinals can eat many times their own weight in a single day.

Birds get their names in different ways. The whip-poor-will gets its name from its cry. So does the bob-white. The cardinal and the bluebird get their names from their color. The woodpeckers get their name because they use their bills to peck wood. The oven-bird gets its name from the kind of nest it builds. The flycatchers catch insects on the wing. And so it goes.

Birds of all kinds lay eggs. Most birds build nests for their eggs. Some build wonderful nests. It is hard to see how they can build such nests without any hands. A bird's eggs must be kept warm for a certain number of days before they will hatch.

Most birds keep their eggs warm by sitting on them. Among many kinds of birds the parents take turns sitting on the nest. Among other kinds of birds only the mother bird sits on the nest. She does not leave the nest except to get food.

The mother hornbill does not leave the nest even for food. A hornbill's nest is in a hollow tree. After the mother bird begins sitting on the eggs, the father bird cements up the entrance to the nest, leaving only a small opening. He then carries food to the mother bird every day. The hornbill is a bird of India.

FISH-EATING BIRDS OF DIFFERENT FAMILIES

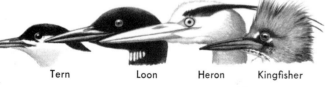

Tern   Loon   Heron   Kingfisher

CLOSELY RELATED BIRDS THAT EAT DIFFERENT FOODS

Shrike   Cardinal   Wood Thrush   Crossbill   Yellowthroat

TYPES OF FEATHERS

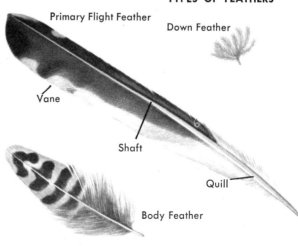

Primary Flight Feather

Down Feather

Vane

Shaft

Quill

Body Feather

The cowbird does not build a nest. The mother bird lays her eggs in the nests of other birds and leaves them there to be hatched. In hot lands a few kinds of birds let the sun hatch their eggs for them.

Some baby birds are naked when they are hatched. Baby robins, for instance, are. They are very helpless, too. Other baby birds are covered with down. Little chickens and ducks are downy babies. They can run about at once.

Different birds eat different kinds of food. From a bird's bill it is sometimes easy to tell what kind of food the bird eats. A

No birds surpass birds of paradise in color.

The helmeted hornbill walls in his mate.

cardinal has a short, stout bill that is good for cracking seeds. A hawk has a sharp, curved bill that is good for tearing apart the animals it catches for food. The hummingbird has a long, slender bill that is good for drinking nectar from flowers. A pelican's bill is very large and makes a good fish basket. No birds, no matter what they eat, have teeth. They grind their food up in their gizzards.

Birds help us in many ways. They eat harmful insects, mice, weed seeds, and dead animals. They furnish us with food. Homing pigeons can be used to carry messages. Cormorants can be trained to help fishermen. Falcons can be trained to help in hunting. Of course, birds also make our lives pleasanter with their bright colors and pretty songs. (See GAME BIRDS; POULTRY; SONGBIRDS; WATER BIRDS.)

BIRDS OF PARADISE No birds in the world have brighter colors than the birds of paradise. From their gay colors no one would guess that they are cousins of our crows.

Many of the feathers of these birds have queer shapes. Some of them make beautiful plumes. Only the male birds have the bright-colored feathers. The females are dull in color.

There are more than 30 kinds of birds of paradise. They live mostly in the hot, rainy forests of the island of New Guinea. A few kinds are found in Australia.

In early times the skins of these birds were used in trading in the East Indies. Travelers from Europe saw them there about 500 years ago. The feet were always cut off the birds before their skins were used. The travelers thought that the birds never had feet. The story was told that these beautiful creatures never stopped flying until they died. Even the famous scientist Linnaeus believed that they had no feet and gave them a scientific name meaning "without feet." As the picture shows, they really have good feet.

Some male birds of paradise, in fact, do a great deal of dancing and strutting about when they are courting. They make dance floors for themselves in the forest.

For a time there was danger that all the birds of paradise would be killed for their feathers. But now laws protect them.

South American Condor

Eagle Owl

Red-tailed Hawk

BIRDS OF PREY The birds pictured on this page are all birds of prey. The best-known birds of prey are the hawks, owls, and eagles. But condors, kites, ospreys, falcons, and vultures belong in the group, too.

No one ever saw an owl picking cherries or an eagle hunting for weed seeds. Birds of prey are all meat eaters. Some eat insects. But most of these birds are so big that they could not easily catch enough insects to live on. They eat larger animals—other birds, fish, frogs, snakes, snails, and mice.

Birds of prey are well fitted to be meat eaters. They have strong, sharp beaks, good for tearing meat. They have strong wings that make it possible for them to swoop down fast on their prey. Most of them have strong feet and sharp claws, good for carrying animals away.

Vultures, however, do not have strong feet and claws. They eat dead animals. A turkey vulture, or turkey buzzard, circling high over a field tells a farmer that there is a dead animal in the field.

Most birds of prey do their hunting during the day. The owls are exceptions. They hunt at night.

Hawks sometimes catch chickens. Eagles have been known to carry away young lambs. Many birds of prey eat smaller birds that help us. But most birds of prey do far more good than harm. They help farmers greatly by killing animals that harm crops. And the vultures are an excellent clean-up brigade.

American Eagle

Osprey

BIRDS OF YESTERDAY Many kinds of birds that once lived on the earth have disappeared. They have, as scientists say, become extinct.

Archaeopteryx (ar kee OP ter iks) is the oldest bird scientists know about. It lived far back in the days of dinosaurs. There have been no birds of this kind for over 100 million years.

This bird has no common name. When it was alive there were no people on earth to give it one. It did not have a name until scientists found fossils of it and studied them. The name the scientists then gave it means "ancient wing."

"Ancient wing" was very different from any bird of today. It had no horny bill. Instead, it had sharp teeth—something no bird of today has. On its wings it had sharp claws. And its tail was much like a lizard's tail even though it had feathers on it. Prob-

Diatryma—A Giant Flightless Bird

ably this ancient bird could not fly very well. It probably climbed about. The claws on its wings may have helped it in climbing.

Archaeopteryx was about the size of a crow. Some of the birds of long ago were much larger. Many of these large birds could not fly. Their wings were too weak to lift them off the ground.

Diatryma (di a TRI ma) was one of the ancient flightless birds. This big bird was as tall as a man. It had stout legs, a large head, and a big beak ending in a sharp hook. Probably *Diatryma* used this hook to tear apart animals it caught. No one ever saw it doing so, for *Diatryma* lived about 50 million years ago — back in the time when horses were the size of fox terriers.

Phororhacos (fo RAHR a kas) was somewhat like *Diatryma*, although it lived about 30 million years later. It, too, was as tall as a man. So big a bird would naturally have a large head, but *Phororhacos* had a bigger head than anyone would expect. It was as big as the head of one of today's horses.

Hesperornis (hes per OR nis) was an ancient water bird. Like *Archaeopteryx*, it

Archaeopteryx had sharp teeth and claws on its wings. It lived more than 100 million years ago.

Hesperornis could not fly but was good at diving for fish.

lived in the days of dinosaurs, but not as long ago as that "ancient wing." It, too, had sharp teeth.

Hesperornis was about four feet long. It had only traces of wings. They do not show at all in the picture. But this big water bird was better fitted for diving than any other bird we know about.

Aepyornis (ee pi OR nis), another big flightless bird, lived during the great Ice Age. Although it is sometimes called an elephant bird, it was really no bigger than an ostrich. But it laid enormous eggs. They were bigger than footballs. A hollow eggshell was big enough to hold a gallon or two of water. Many fossil eggshells have been found on the island of Madagascar.

The tallest birds anyone knows about were moas. Some were no larger than turkeys, but some grew to be 11 feet tall. Of course, they could not fly. Unlike some of the flightless birds of past ages, the moas had small heads.

The moas lived in New Zealand. They did not disappear so very long ago. The early natives probably helped cause these birds to become extinct by killing them for meat. What a dinner an 11-foot moa must have made!

People also played a part in making the dodo disappear. The dodo lived on two islands in the Indian Ocean. It was killed off by men, pigs, and monkeys. The dodo has been extinct for about 300 years.

Some birds have become extinct within the last century. The great auk is one of them. This bird looked like a penguin. It could swim well, but it could not fly.

Great auks built their nests on islands near the eastern shores of North America. At nesting time they were caught and carried away from the islands by the boatload. Now there are none left.

The passenger pigeon is another bird that became extinct not long ago. Unless we protect them, some of the birds of today are sure to disappear. (See CONSERVA-TION; DINOSAURS; DODO; LIFE THROUGH THE AGES; MAMMALS OF YESTERDAY; PASSENGER PIGEON.)

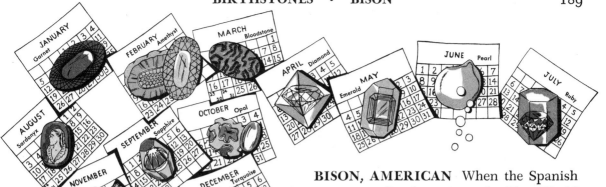

BIRTHSTONES

From very early times there have been superstitions about precious stones. Long ago some stones were supposed to make anyone who wore them strong and brave. Others were supposed to protect their wearers from fire and lightning. Still others were supposed to bring good health and good fortune.

The idea of birthstones came from these old superstitions. Each month was given a stone. Wearing this stone, people thought, would bring good fortune to anyone whose birthday was in the month.

Not many people still have the old idea that precious stones can help or harm them. But many people do enjoy wearing their birthstones.

Not everyone agrees about what the birthstone for each month is. One grouping that is often followed is shown above. (See DIAMONDS; GEMS; PEARLS.)

BISON, AMERICAN

When the Spanish conqueror Cortés came to the New World more than 400 years ago, he found in the zoo of the Aztec king a big animal which he thought very strange. One of his men wrote that this animal looked as if it were made up of parts of several different animals. It had a bunch of hair on its back like a camel, its neck was covered with hair like a lion, and its head was armed like a bull's. It had, besides, crooked shoulders, a large tail, and hoofs. It was fierce and strong. Cortés called the animal a Mexican bull. It was an American bison.

Many people call American bison buffaloes, but bison are not true buffaloes. True buffaloes are cousins of the domestic ox and are found only in Asia and Africa. They do not have the big arched shoulders and shaggy hair of the bison.

Less than a hundred years ago there were enormous herds of wild bison on the Great Plains of America. In all the herds together there were millions of animals. The first white settlers to cross the plains were in danger of being killed by stampedes of these big animals.

But as the West was settled, the bison were killed by the thousands. Many were killed for meat and for their hides. Others were killed just for the fun of hunting. The last great bison hunt was in 1883. Then a thousand animals were killed.

When the American government realized that all the bison would soon be gone, it set aside some places where the dwindling herds could live in safety. Now there are more than 20,000 bison in herds on these reservations. There are bison in many zoos, too. (See BUFFALO BILL.)

The Black Death terrified all of Europe.

BLACK DEATH In the 14th century a terrible disease spread over Europe. It was called the Black Death. Millions of people died of it.

There are many stories of the Black Death. Some tell of ghost ships that drifted about with all members of the crews dead. Some tell of beggars who stole gold and jewels from the dead and became very rich — but only for a day. There are other stories even more unpleasant.

One of the great doctors of the Middle Ages blamed the Black Death on Jupiter, Saturn, and Mars. These three planets, he said, were too close together in the sky. Now we know that the Black Death was caused by germs which fleas carried from rats to people.

The disease has not yet been stamped out. Today it is called bubonic plague. It is still terrible, but we know how to fight against it.

Fighting it means chiefly fighting rats and fleas. In our harbors we try to keep rats from coming ashore from ships. They might be bringing in bubonic plague. (See DISEASE GERMS.)

BLACK SEA The Black Sea separates eastern Europe and Asia Minor. Ships travel between it and the Mediterranean Sea through the Bosporus, the Sea of Marmara, and the Dardanelles.

Four countries have shores on the Black Sea. They are Turkey, Rumania, Bulgaria, and the Soviet Union. Their shores on the Black Sea are the only seacoasts Rumania and Bulgaria have. The Soviet Union's Black Sea shore is not her only seacoast, but it is a very important one. On it are her only warm water ports. Her northern ports are often blocked for several months during the winter by ice.

The famous Danube River flows into the Black Sea. So do two big Russian rivers, the Dnieper (NEE per) and the Don. The large amount of fresh water from these rivers makes the Black Sea less salty than the Mediterranean. (See BOSPORUS; DARDANELLES; STRAIT.)

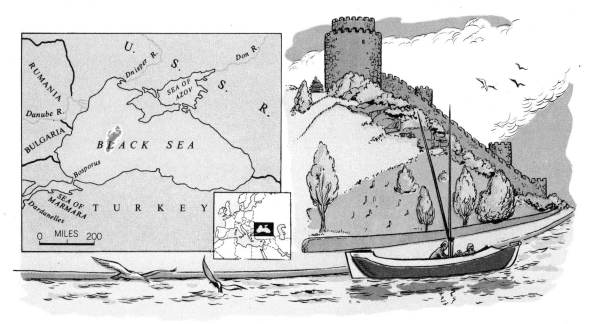

BLARNEY STONE If a person says a great many pleasant things that he doesn't really mean, someone may say, "Oh, he must have kissed the Blarney Stone." The Blarney Stone is a stone high in the wall of Blarney Castle, an ancient, ruined castle near the city of Cork in Ireland. The date 1446 was carved into the stone. Long ago the idea spread that if a person kissed the Blarney Stone he would become very clever at saying flattering things.

No one believes now that the Blarney Stone has any real power. But every year many tourists go to see the castle. Some of them kiss the Blarney Stone just for the fun of saying that they have done so.

Kissing the Blarney Stone is not easy. First a person must climb to the very top of the castle. Then he has to be held so that he can hang upside down over the stone railing there. Many people decide to be satisfied with kissing some other stone in the wall. (See SUPERSTITIONS.)

BLIZZARD A snowstorm may be rather pleasant. Big flakes may drift slowly down. But a snowstorm is not always pleasant. The snow may be driven by a very cold, strong wind. A heavy snowstorm with a strong wind is called a blizzard. Many travelers have lost their way in the blinding snow of a blizzard and died from the cold. Many horses and cattle out on range have frozen to death in blizzards, too. The famous blizzard of 1888 killed more than

Range horses huddle in a blizzard.

After the blizzard: drifts and broken wires.

200 people in New York City. For three days it snowed steadily and the wind blew fiercely. In places the snow drifted 10 feet high. (See STORMS; WEATHER.)

BLOOD To stay alive our bodies have to have food and oxygen. But just having food in our stomachs does no good. Just having oxygen in our lungs does no good, either. The food and the oxygen must be carried to the ends of our noses and the tips of our toes and to every other part of our bodies.

Our blood does the carrying. It travels in tubes called blood vessels. The heart pumps the blood through them.

The blood does even more than carry food and oxygen. Its work is so important that the heart has to keep pumping it day in and day out without ever stopping to rest.

A person who weighs 100 pounds has about four quarts of blood. Bigger people have more. Smaller people have less.

A drop of blood looks like a drop of red ink. But it is much, much more compli-

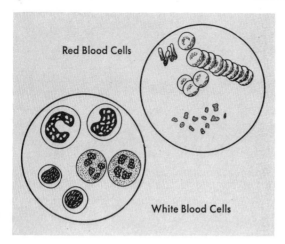

Red Blood Cells

White Blood Cells

cated. The liquid part of our blood is not red. Blood looks red because it has many tiny red cells in it. Red cells are far too small to be seen without a microscope. It would take thousands of them to make a row an inch long. Everyone has billions of red cells in his blood.

The chief work of the red cells is to carry oxygen. They gather it in the lungs and take it to all the other cells of the body.

Red blood cells are made inside some of our bones. Millions of new ones are made every second of our lives. But millions of worn-out red cells are destroyed every second, too. They are destroyed in the liver and in the spleen.

There are also white cells of several kinds in our blood. Those of one kind make up an army to fight disease germs. They really eat the disease germs up. Those of another kind help repair parts of the body that have been damaged by germs. There are usually one or two white cells for every 1,000 red cells.

The liquid part of the blood is called plasma. It is mostly water. But the water has many important chemicals dissolved in it. It has, for instance, one chemical that makes blood grow thick, or clot. It has another that keeps it from clotting when it shouldn't. It has chemicals that help keep our bodies working as they should. There are other chemicals that help the white cells fight germs.

It is the plasma that carries food to all parts of the body. The plasma also gathers up waste materials and carries them to the lungs or the skin or the kidneys so that they can be got rid of.

It is easy to see that a drop of blood as it rushes through our bodies is always changing. Here it picks up oxygen. There it picks up food. Here it leaves some food. Here it leaves some oxygen. Here it gathers up some waste. Here it leaves a company of white cells to fight some germs that have got into a cut. Here it picks up a chemical. There it leaves it. Round and round it travels, like a delivery boy that works 24 hours a day every day.

People are not the only animals with blood. All animals with backbones have blood. So do many animals without backbones. Only simple animals can get along without it. (See BODY, HUMAN; CELLS; HEART; PHYSIOLOGY.)

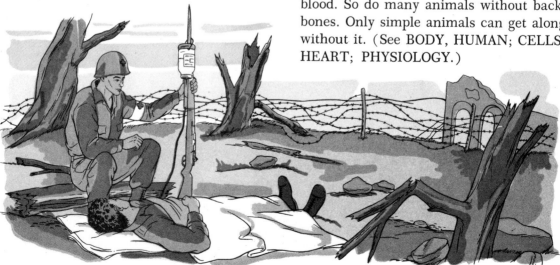

A soldier gives blood plasma to a wounded man on the battlefield.

THE GOLDEN BOOK ENCYCLOPEDIA

CONTAINS THE FOLLOWING VOLUMES

CONTRIBUTING ARTISTS

Dot and Sy Barlowe • Cornelius De Witt • E. Joseph Dreany • Bruno Frost
James Gordon Irving • Beth and Joe Krush • Harry Lazarus • Andre LeBlanc
H. Charles McBarron • Denny McMains • Harry McNaught
Ray Perlman • John Polgreen • Evelyn Urbanowich

Pauline Batchelder Adams • George Avison • Barry Bart • Ernie Barth • Charles Bellow
Eric Bender • Juanita Bennett • Merrit Berger • Robert D. Bezucha • William Bolin
Thelma Bowie • Matilda Breuer • S. Syd Brown • Peter Buchard • Louise Fulton Bush
Jim Caraway • Nino Carbe • Sam Citron • Gordon Clifton • Mel Crawford • Robert Doremus
Harry Daugherty • Rachel Taft Dixon • Olive Earle • Sydney F. Fletcher • F. Beaumont Fox
Rudolf Freund • Tibor Gergely • Douglas Gorsline • Hamilton Greene • Gerald Gregg
Marjorie Hartwell • Hans H. Helweg • Janice Holland • W. Ben Hunt
Arch and Miriam Hurford • Harper Johnson • Norman Jonsson • Matthew Kalmenoff
Janet Robson Kennedy • Paul Kinnear • Olga Kucera • Walter Kumme • John Leone
Kenneth E. Lowman • John Alan Maxwell • Jean McCammack • Shane Miller • Stina Nagel
Elizabeth Newhall • Gregory Orloff • Raymond Pease • Alice and Martin Provensen
Jerry Robinson • Feodor Rojankovsky • Roki • Mary Royt • Arnold W. Ryan
Arthur Sanford • Sam Savitts • William Sayles • Al Schmidt • Edwin Schmidt
Frederick E. Seyfarth • Robert Sherman • George Solonewitsch • Lionel Stern
Norton Stewart • Valerie Swenson • Gustaf Tenggren • William Thompson • Felix Traugott
Eileen Fox Vaughn • Herschel Wartik • Robert Weisman • Garth Williams

MAPS BY

Vincent Kotschar   Jean Paul Tremblay
Carol Vinall   Frederic Lorenzen
Rudolf von Siegl   Francis Barkoczy

COVER ARTISTS

Ned Seidler • Ken Davies • Don Moss